LOST TRACKS

NATIONAL BUFFALO PARK, 1909–1939

Lost Tracks

NATIONAL BUFFALO PARK, 1909–1939

by Jennifer Brower

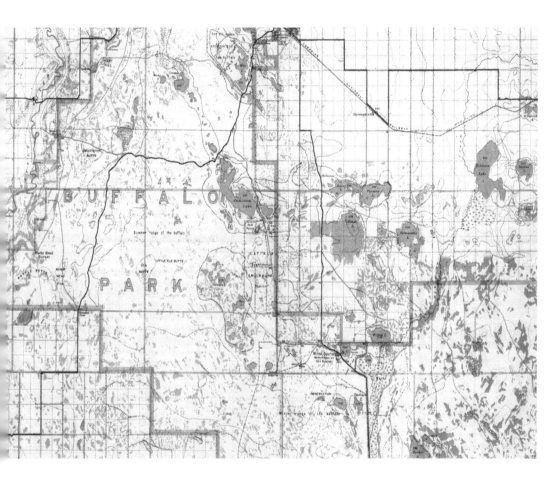

AU PRESS

Published by AU Press, Athabasca University
1200, 10011 – 109 Street
Edmonton, AB T5J 3S8

Library and Archives Canada Cataloguing in Publication

Brower, Jennifer, 1974-
      Lost tracks : Buffalo National Park, 1909-1939 / Jennifer Brower.

Also available in electronic format.
Includes bibliographical references and index.
ISBN 978-1-897425-10-7

      1. Buffalo National Park (Alta.)–History. 2. American bison–Conservation–
Alberta–Buffalo National Park. I. Title.

FC3664.B84B76 2008
C2008-902814-7
971.23'02

Printed and bound in Canada by AGMV Marquis

Book design and layout by Willa Kung
Cover design by Helen Adhikari
Cover artwork by Dara Humniski

The photographs and maps in the book are courtesy of the following sources or institutions:

Dwight Allott: p. 148 – map created from public domain source; Battle River Historical
Society: p. 139; Buffalo National Park Foundation Archives: p. 70, p. 137: Rutherford Fonds;
Denise Ens: p. 15 – map created from public domain source; Glenbow Archives: p. 3: NA-1590-4;
p. 22: NA-1792-3-4; National Resources Canada: p. iii, p. 20; Herb Snyder: p. 110, p. 134;
Royal Geographic Society: p. 18; Ellis Treffry: p. 57; p. 59; p. 72; p. 91, p. 106

This book was funded in part by the Alberta Historical Resources Foundation.

Contents

Acknowledgements

My interest in the history of Buffalo National Park was first inspired by the stories told to me by Jean Brower, my grandmother, and by Ray Sharp, one of the Park Rangers at BNP. Through my research for this book, which started as an MA thesis, I have met many others whose stories deepened my interest in this park and its history. Thank you to those who granted me interviews and allowed me to use their photographs for this book.

Sincere thanks to my thesis supervisor, Dr. Gerhard Ens, for his guidance and support. Many others offered thoughtful critiques and advice along the way, for which I am grateful. Last, thank you to my parents, Keith and Aileen, my family, and my husband Bevan for their support and encouragement.

Jennifer Brower
Wainwright, Alberta
May 1, 2008

Introduction

> It is a melancholy contemplation for one who has travelled as I have, through these realms, and seen this noble animal in all its pride and glory, to contemplate it so rapidly wasting from the world, drawing the irresistible conclusion too, which one must do, that its species is soon to be extinguished…
>
> And what a splendid contemplation too, when one (who has travelled these realms, and can duly appreciate them) imagines them as they *might* in the future be seen (by some great protecting policy of government) preserved in their pristine beauty and wildness, in a *magnificent park*…What a beautiful and thrilling specimen for America to preserve and hold up to the view of her refined citizens and the world, in future ages! A *nation's Park*, containing man and beast, in all the wild and freshness of their nature's beauty![1]

The artist George Catlin wrote these stirring words in 1832 while close to present-day South Dakota. He detested the wasteful exploitation of the plains bison and cried out for a place where they and the Aboriginal peoples who relied on them could be preserved.[2]

Catlin's plea, however, fell on deaf ears. Instead, the 19th century witnessed the near destruction of the plains bison, popularly known as "buffalo," whose numbers on the North American Plains had once reached thirty million.[3] The Canadian government came closest to realizing Catlin's dream. In 1906, Sir Wilfrid Laurier's Liberal administration negotiated to purchase what was considered the largest and last free-ranging plains bison herd on the continent from Montana rancher Michel Pablo. In 1908, the government established Buffalo Park Reserve, later called Buffalo National Park, near Wainwright, Alberta to save and increase the near-extinct species.

Most historians who have studied Buffalo National Park have viewed the purchase of the Pablo bison herd and its management as a great wildlife preservation effort. However, they have made this classification and based their conclusions on a very short period of the park's history—the purchase years (1907–1912).[4] On closer investigation, however, and when the entire park history is considered, a very different story emerges. The turn of the century meaning of the term "preservation" can be equated with what would now be defined as "conservation," or the "planned and efficient use of natural resources to ensure their permanence."[5] The two terms were often used interchangeably. Even in light of this, Buffalo National Park cannot be considered a wildlife preservation effort.[6] Rather, Buffalo National Park was an artefact defined and shaped by the cultural, political, and economic climate of early 20th century Canada. These forces influenced the establishment and directed the management of this park, and ultimately played the biggest role in its demise.

At one time, the range of the plains bison extended over one-third of the North American continent. The bison were found from the Atlantic coast to the Great Plains, the environment in which they flourished. Their range extended southward to the delta of the Mississippi, westward across Texas to northeastern Mexico and across the Rocky Mountains into New Mexico, Utah, and Idaho. In Canada, a few bison were found in British Columbia; most ranged in the plains west of the Canadian Shield to the Rocky Mountains.[7] While Hornaday stated the northern range of the bison extended to the shores of Great Slave Lake, he may have been referring to the wood bison, another subspecies of bison that differs slightly in structure and pelage and is larger than its plains counterpart.[8]

By the mid-1880s, however, the plains bison was on the brink of extinction. Several factors diminished the bison population even before the systematic slaughter began around 1820. Settlement in the east had pushed nearly all of the population west of the Mississippi River. Advances in the native culture, such as the introduction of the horse, had allowed hunters to be more selective. Cows were chosen because their meat was more palatable and their hides thinner and lighter. By the 1800s, the population of bison on the south plains was noticeably reduced.[9]

Competition in the fur trade also accelerated the pressure on the population. The first organized hunt on a grand scale took place in 1820 out of Red River. While at one time herds ranged near the Red River settlement, the bison were driven back as the Métis started an annual summer hunt to

Park Riders traverse exposed sand dunes in Buffalo National Park.

harvest hides and to provide meat and pemmican for employees of the Hudson's Bay Company. The American Fur Company dominated the fur trade in the western plains and the eastern robe market. The invention of steam-powered riverboats allowed the American Fur Company to reach the Upper Missouri and steamships allowed a greater quantity of bison robes to be shipped cheaply. By 1840, 100,000 bison robes were harvested per year.[10]

The overhunting of the bison accelerated in the 1870s and early 1880s due to the demands of eastern markets and an increasingly industrial society. The completion of the Union Pacific Railway in 1869 across the mid-United States from Omaha, Nebraska to Promontory Summit, Utah, divided the plains bison into two great herds, the northern herd and the southern herd, and accelerated the destruction of the bison by two decades. Pressure on the southern herd accelerated with introduction of the Sharps Big 50, a more powerful rifle that allowed hunters to fire more accurately, and the development, by 1870, of a method to make industrial belts from bison hides. Steam locomotives transported bison hides to the eastern markets more efficiently. After the hunt of 1875, the great southern herd ceased to exist. Only scattered bands of bison survived.

On the northern plains, environmental conditions, especially drought, and competition for rangeland with domestic cattle also contributed to the demise of the bison in the latter half of the 1800s. Both native and European hide hunters put pressure on the northern herd, and hunting accelerated once the southern herd had collapsed. By 1879 only a few bison were left in Canada. The last significant hunt occurred in 1882–1883, after which the plains bison was almost extinct. By the 1890s, there were no wild plains bison left on the Canadian Prairies and only small pockets of animals remained on the American Plains.[11]

Five individual efforts have been credited with saving the plains bison from extinction. James McKay and Charles Alloway of Manitoba, Charles Goodnight of Texas, Samuel Walking Coyote of Montana, Frederick Dupree of South Dakota, and Charles "Buffalo" Jones of Kansas all captured bison calves when it became clear that the species, without some intervention, would disappear from the Great Plains. The lineage of most bison alive today can be traced to these herds. Montana native Samuel Walking Coyote captured calves, as outlined in a well-reported legend, as a gift to appease the priests at St. Ignatius over the problems of his second, illicit, marriage.[12] Walking Coyote sold his bison herd to ranchers Charles Allard and Michel Pablo in 1883, when his herd had increased to twelve animals.[13] The herd continued to increase on its new range in the Flathead Valley of Montana and by 1896, the year Allard died, it numbered approximately 300 animals. Allard's half of the herd was dispersed among his wife and children and sold to various buyers.[14] Pablo continued to graze his bison until the United States government applied the *Dawes Act* in the Flathead Valley, in 1904. This act allowed tribe members to select a homestead of 160 acres and opened the remainder of the valley for settlement, which forced Pablo to find a new range for his bison.[15] In 1907, the Dominion Government purchased Pablo's plains bison herd, and soon afterward created Buffalo National Park.

Alan MacEachern writes that the history of national parks needs to be viewed through a cultural looking glass. Everything about a national park, from the choice of a location to the park's subsequent management is based on a variety of "aesthetic, economic, and political reasons."[16] As I hope this case study will prove, all decisions—from the purchase of the bison herd, the establishment and location of the park, to the policies that dictated the management of the bison—were defined and shaped by the cultural atmosphere of the early 20th century and contributed to the downfall of Buffalo National Park.

A number of cumulative factors contributed to Buffalo National Park's failure as a bison-saving effort. The park area, chosen because it was considered useless as agricultural land, ultimately could not sustain an overgrown bison herd. The misguided motives of those in the Dominion government who negotiated the purchase overshadowed any preservationist considerations for the bison. Sentiment for the nearly extinct species and a wish to show up the Americans by purchasing the herd propelled these individuals rather than an interest in actually saving the species. Those administrating the effort, first in the Department of the Interior and soon after, the Parks Branch, knew little about managing wildlife when the park was established and this had a negative impact on the effort. In the first decade, little thought was given to the consequences of the burgeoning herd until it was too late. By the 1920s, the park was experiencing an overpopulation problem that led to the degradation of the range and the spread of disease, of which tuberculosis was the most serious. Environmental factors, such as drought in the 1920s and the Great Depression of the 1930s, also took their toll on the effort.

While these cultural influences contributed to the problems that Buffalo National Park experienced almost immediately after its formation, the economic strain that resulted from the lack of federal funding resulted in poor management decisions which escalated the problems into crises. While the

Dominion government had backed the purchase and the establishment of the park financially and wholeheartedly, it did not show the same dedication to supporting the park's operations. The Parks Branch, the small branch of the Department of the Interior that administrated the park, was not given the financial resources to operate it effectively. As the crises at the park escalated, the Parks Branch was obligated to find temporary measures to delay the mounting problems. Inevitably, the focus of their management became profiting from the bison just to sustain the park itself. However, the Parks Branch was not successful even at realizing much profit. Without significant funding, the conditions of the park could not be improved. Ultimately, the government that established the park did not have the resolve to follow through with the effort.

Notes

1. Roderick Nash, ed., *The American Environment: Readings in the History of Conservation* (Massachusetts 1968), 8–9. Emphasis in original.

2. Nash, *American Environment*, 7–9.

3. Dale Lott believes that the North American Plains could have supported only thirty million bison prior to the over hunting of the species in the latter half of the 19th century. See Dale Lott, *American Bison: A Natural History* (Berkeley 2002), 69–76, 170.

4. Coder, Foster, and Ogilvie all present Buffalo National Park as a preservationist effort. Coder's and Foster's studies look only at the purchase years and do not treat Buffalo National Park's changing policies and the results. However, even Sheilagh Ogilvie, who has examined the role of Buffalo National Park in protecting and increasing the bison herds in the national parks system, and who acknowledged the problems the management faced, has defined the effort as preservationist. George David Coder, "The National Movement to Preserve the American Buffalo in the United States and Canada Between 1880 and 1920," PhD diss., (Ohio State University, 1975); Janet Foster, *Working for Wildlife: The Beginning of Preservation in Canada*, 2nd ed. (Toronto 1998); and Sheilagh C. Ogilvie, *The Park Buffalo* (Calgary 1979).

5. Alan MacEachern, "The Conservation Movement," in *Canada, Confederation to Present* [CD-ROM]. Bob Hesketh and Chris Hackett eds. (Edmonton 2001).

6. MacEachern, "Conservation Movement," endnote 2. Gordon Hewitt's book, *The Conservation of the Wildlife of Canada*, is a good example of how the terms preservation and conservation were used synonymously. See, for example, C. Gordon Hewitt, *The Conservation of the Wildlife of Canada* (New York 1921), 7.

7. William Temple Hornaday, *The Extermination of the American Bison* (Washington 2002), 376-377, 384.

8. Hornaday, *Extermination*, 376–377, 384. "Natural Wonders & Cultural Treasures," *Elk Island National Park of Canada* <http://www2.parkscanada. gc.ca/pn-np/ab/elkisland/natcul/natcul1biii_E.asp> (30 March 2008).

9. Hornaday, *Extermination*, 487; Lott, *American Bison*, 171–72.

10. Lott, *American Bison*, 105, 173–74; Hornaday, *Extermination*, 487–88; Andrew C. Isenberg, *The Destruction of the Bison* (Cambridge 2000), 93–94.

11. Hornaday, *Extermination*, 505–07; Lott, *American Bison*, 175, 179; Isenberg, *Destruction*, 141–43; Ogilvie, *Park Buffalo*, 7–8.

12. Coder, "National Movement," 15–23. For a detailed account of the oral traditions concerning the events surrounding the Walking Coyote bison calves, see Bon I. Whealdon et al., *I Will Be Meat for My Salish* (Pablo 2001), chapters 4–5.

13. Coder, "National Movement," 22. However, other accounts claim the year to be 1884. See Whealdon et al., *I Will Be Meat for My Salish*, 82.

14. Charles Allard's wife sold her portion of the estate to Charles E. Conrad of Kalispell, Montana. Howard Eaton also purchased some bison from Allard's estate. A portion of these were later bought by Donald A. Smith, Lord Strathcona, and presented to the Dominion government. Whealdon et al., *I Will Be Meat for My Salish*, 87.

15. Lott, *American Bison*, 188; "Flathead Reservation Timeline," *Flathead Reservation Historical Society*, Montana Heritage Project, 2004 <http://www.flatheadreservation.org/timeline/timeline.html> (14 June 2004).

16. Alan MacEachern, *Natural Selections: National Parks in Atlantic Canada* (Montreal 2001), 4.

CHAPTER ONE

Where the Buffalo Roamed

*Perceptions of the Neutral Hills Landscape and
the Creation of Buffalo National Park*

PRIOR TO THE MID-19TH CENTURY, THE GEOGRAPHY of the Canadian West was largely unknown to those living outside the region. Prompted by a growing expansionist view of the Canadian North West, however, the 1860s expeditions by Captain John Palliser and Henry Youle Hind and later surveys by Naturalist John Macoun helped redefine the region.[1] They found much of the Canadian West favourable for settlement. Palliser, however, explored the Neutral Hills area and had little optimism for the potential of the land that would one day become Buffalo National Park. The Dominion land surveyors that followed at the turn of the 20th century also found the land south of Wainwright useless for settlement and agricultural purposes.

While perceived by Palliser and the Dominion Land Surveyors to be inferior for agricultural uses, the area north of the Neutral Hills had historically sustained large bison herds. This fact was influential in the establishment of Buffalo National Park. In 1907, the Dominion government sent Homestead Inspector Joseph Bannerman to examine the area south of Wainwright, Alberta, for use as a potential bison reserve. "[W]hile undesirable as agricultural land," Bannerman found this tract to be "eminently suitable for the purpose intended, being well supplied with water and grazing."[2] He recommended the land for a new park.[3] This impression, however, was uninformed. With the onset of settlement, the face of the Canadian West had changed. Very quickly, those involved in the administration of the park would find that the intricate relationship between the bison and the parkland environment was not easily understood.

John Palliser, the son of an elite Irish landowner, and Henry Youle Hind, a geologist contracted by the Canadian government, were both on a mission to explore the Canadian West in search of its potential for resources and, ultimately, for settlement. Palliser, leader of a British expedition funded by the Royal Geographical Society, explored British North America from 1857 to 1860 and Hind led two Canadian expeditions into the interior in 1857 and 1858.[4]

The Palliser expedition was most influential for categorizing the area in the North West into specific districts based on soil fertility. Palliser conceptualized the existence of a "fertile belt" and a desert area in the Canadian Plains, which he outlined in his general report. Hind's report, published in 1860, also incorporated these concepts.[5] Palliser located good land along the valley of the North Saskatchewan and land of poorer quality in the plains to the south. The poorest area occurred where the central desert in the United States extended north of the 49th parallel and formed a small triangle of arid land.[6] Generally, Palliser deemed the land along the Battle River, some of which would be eventually chosen for Buffalo National Park, to be good for the pasturage of livestock. He wrote in his general report:

> The richness of the natural pasture in many places on the prairies of the second level along the North Saskatchewan and its tributary, the Battle River, can hardly be exaggerated. Its value does not consist in its being rank or in great quantity, but from its fine quality, comprising nutritious species of grasses and carices, along with natural vetches in great variety, which remain throughout the winter sound, juicy, and fit for the nourishment of stock.[7]

While Hind never explored as far as the area that would later become Buffalo National Park,[8] it appears from the description in the *Papers of the Palliser Expedition* that Palliser passed as close as five to ten miles from the southern border of the park. In a report to the Royal Geographical Society of London, Palliser's impression of the park area was more negative. He had little to report on the region until he reached Flag Hill, west of the Battle River near present-day Hardisty. In recounting the progress of the expedition through this area, he wrote, "I will not occupy your Lordship's time with minute details of our journey from this [Grand Coulée to the Battle River], as the prairie was neither well provided with wood nor rich in pasture, but will pass on to the period of our arrival at the Battle River."[9] This finding strengthened Palliser's negative view of the land's potential. According to Irene Spry's descriptions of Palliser's 1859 map of the North West, the park would have fallen within the "fertile belt." However, in the 1860 and 1865 maps, the northern border of the arid regions, or "true prairie," had been moved farther north and west.[10] Perhaps the discovery of inferior land, such as the tract found by Palliser in the vicinity of the park, motivated changes in the area defined as the fertile belt on these subsequent maps.

The influence of Palliser's theory of a fertile belt and a desert triangle is evident in the years following his expedition as his theory appeared in literature about the region. Commissioned by the Canadian government to gather information about conditions in the North West Territories in 1870, William Francis Butler was certainly aware of Palliser and used his theory when describing the "land of the Saskatchewan":

> Its boundaries are of the simplest description…It has on the north a huge forest, on the west a huge mountain, on the south an immense desert, on the east an immense marsh. From the forest to the desert there lies a distance varying from 40 to 150 miles, and from the marsh to the mountain, 800 miles of land lie spread in every varying phase of undulating fertility. This is the Fertile Belt, the land of the Saskatchewan, the winter home of the buffalo, the war country of the Crees and Blackfeet, the future home of millions yet unborn.[11]

Palliser's theory was so influential that, as the North West began to be considered for settlement, it became necessary to downplay the desert image of the southern Plains. Instead a utopian view of agricultural fertility was promoted, as can be seen in the following excerpt from an 1887 brochure on the North West:

> Much the greatest part of these vast prairies possesses a soil of astonishing fertility, and even in regions less favoured in this respect, there are no great extents as stated by Capt. Palliser, in his report to the Imperial Government, at all approaching to sterility…even in that strip heretofore designated 'the desert' there is comparatively but a small part of the land unfit for the culture of the cereals or for pasture.[12]

This optimism might be attributed to the fact that the Plains experienced exceptionally wet years from the mid-1870s to the early 1880s, when the Dominion Land Surveyors were mapping the area for settlement.[13] Near the Squirrel Hills, the area Palliser reported as the "northern extension of the North American arid basin,"[14] John Macoun, a naturalist who conducted several surveying expeditions of the North West from 1872 to 1881, found the land more favourable than Palliser had reported. After nine years of study, he believed that the climate of the Canadian prairies was influenced by the Great American Desert, which resulted in a generally drier climate but a warm summer with an abundance of rain. He praised the fertility of the soil that extended over the boundless region and concluded, "our great North-West is truly a land of 'illimitable possibilities.'"[15]

While Dominion land surveyors favourably documented the southern arid regions, this same confidence is certainly not reflected in the reports of the surveyors who went through the Wainwright region. Both the first block surveys in 1883 and 1884 and the township surveys in 1903 were very candid about the land's unsuitability for settlement.[16] While the field notes from the first block surveys did not include a written report of the area, Tom Kains, leader of one of the 1883 surveying parties, kept a diary recording his expedition's movements and brief comments on the weather and topography. On 1 June, he took notice of the poor soil and wrote, "Sandy Country with growth of stunted poplar."[17] James F. Garden, another surveyor who charted most of the park area, also found sand to be the most prevalent component of the soil. In some areas he even encountered sand ridges.[18] Garden surveyed the area around Ribstone Creek and also found it to be very sandy.[19] Only along the muskeg areas of the Ribstone was the soil found to be wet mould or loam above alkaline clay.[20] Despite the area's sandiness, the flourishing vegetation is surprising. Garden noted dense continuous poplar trees, up to ten inches in diametre, and Balm of Gilead trees growing on a soil of sand.[21]

While the 1883 and 1884 surveys only mapped the township borders, the 1903 surveys charted and appraised each individual section in the township. Surveyor field notes could not be located for the entire park area, but the information recorded in the existing field notes does not deviate from either the general impressions of Palliser or those of the earlier block surveyors. Except for the Ribstone Creek area, surveyors C. C. Fairchild and M. B. Weekes found the park area to be very sandy and unfit for agricultural purposes.[22] Weekes even expressed reservations about township 44, range 8, one that seemed to have some of the better soil in the park area. He wrote, "This township is not suitable for anything except ranching, and is not very well adapted for that as the grass is not very good."[23]

While the area south of Wainwright was considered unfit for agriculture and settlement, it was well known by those living in, visiting, or exploring the Canadian West that the area was suitable for game, especially bison. John Warkentin notes that traders knew that the land on the North Saskatchewan was more fertile than the Wainwright region farther south, yet they never associated this poorer land with a "desert wasteland" because the region was

This map, compiled from surveyor's observations found in Dominion Land Surveyors records from 1883–1884 and 1903, shows that much of the Buffalo National Park landscape consisted of sandy soil, of which a large area was sand dunes.

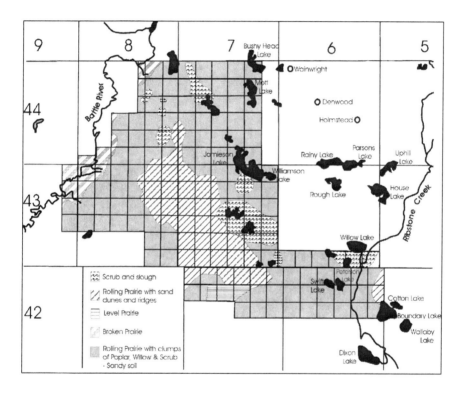

known to produce numerous bison.[24] Indeed, vast herds of plains bison had been observed by many explorers that passed through the area. In 1754, Anthony Henday, somewhere near the Alberta/Saskatchewan border, west-southwest of Battleford, encountered "buffalo grazing like English cattle." A few days later and not far from that place, he jotted the following observation: "the Buffalo so numerous obliged to make them sheer out of the way."[25] Palliser also described bison in large numbers in the vicinity of the park. Near Ribstone Creek, he stated, "As the buffalos were very numerous, regulations were made to economize our ammunition, and to prevent the useless killing of animals."[26]

These perceptions reflect what archaeologists and historians today know about the region. Buffalo National Park, located in this parkland belt south of the North Saskatchewan and in the vicinity of the Battle River, was an area where the bison, and thus Natives, wintered. Environmental historian Theodore Binnema notes that "bison concentrations varied seasonally according to regular patterns under normal conditions and in predictable ways under anomalous conditions."[27] The "fescue crescent," the broad parkland belt that runs near the North Saskatchewan River and encompasses the rough terrain of the foothills, was the traditional wintering grounds for the plains bison. The bison wintered in this northern prairie from September until the spring as it afforded the best forage and shelter to survive the winter.[28] Archaeologist J. Roderick Vickers has suggested that the natives who wintered in parklands from November/December to March subsisted on "stalking and communal hunting of bison."[29] Archaeologist George Arthur affirms that "northern Plains tribes used the traditional jumps and pounds from late fall throughout the winter and also at other times of the year."[30]

Not only were bison important for sustaining Native populations, but their migratory behaviour was also important in renewing the landscape. George Arthur argues that many of the bison's behavioural habits, while they appeared destructive, benefited the land. Under normal conditions, trampling (the heavy treading of the bison on the landscape) encouraged the growth of vegetation by prompting the reseeding of natural grasses, and helped to reduce water loss from the soil. Even though wallowing destroyed ground cover, it also created hollows that collected water after other moisture sources dried up. Uprooting or breaking trees by rubbing helped maintain the grassland by keeping trees, specifically aspen, from establishing themselves.[31]

Wild animals, particularly bison, flourished in the park area because it was in the vicinity of a tribal boundary between the Blackfoot and the

Cree. A "commons" system existed on the North American Plains before the arrival of the Europeans; it had well-recognized tribal boundaries, separated by neutral areas.[32] Just south of Buffalo National Park, the Neutral Hills were a natural, recognized boundary between the Blackfoot to the southwest and the Cree to the northeast.[33] James Hector, the naturalist and geologist with Palliser's expedition, gave a description of the border between these two tribes: "In the latitude of Fort Ellice they sometimes pitch their tents as far west as the Elbow of the South Saskatchewan, and from that point their country may be bounded by a line carried to the Neutral hills, south of Battle River, and thence on to the Beaver hills and Fort Edmonton."[34]

Paul Martin and Christine Szuter's research has revealed that the existence of war zones had a greater impact in determining the size of game animal populations than the quality of vegetation or natural conditions. In the North American context, Martin and Szuter have found that wildlife flourished along the tribal boundary lines separating two hostile tribes because such areas were too dangerous for either tribe to penetrate.[35] During Meriwether Lewis and William Clark's exploration in the United States east of the Rockies, Clark commented on this phenomenon: "I have observed that in the country between the nations which are at war with each other the greatest numbers of wild animals are to be found."[36]

Palliser's observations show a similar occurrence of plentiful wild animals at the boundary between the Blackfoot and the Cree. His notes contain numerous references to the hostilities between these two tribes.[37] The Cree, aware that animal populations thrived between war zones, informed the Palliser expedition on one occasion that they were "not more than two days' journey off from plenty of buffalo out westward; but they said they did not like to go so far, as they would then be in the enemy's country."[38] Three days later, Palliser recorded encountering bison after entering the neutral area between the Cree and the Blackfoot.[39] Proof of the wealth of plains bison in the Wainwright area is perhaps best displayed on a map that accompanied the *Papers of the Palliser Expedition*; "Great herds of Buffalo" is written on the map across the area between the Battle River and the Neutral Hills, right in the vicinity of Buffalo National Park.[40] The area was a haven for bison long before the Canadian government established a reserve for them.

Creating a park for bison seemed an ideal use for this otherwise useless land. North America has a long history of establishing national parks in areas considered unusable for agriculture and development. Alfred Runte

A portion of the "General Map of Routes in British North America Explored by the Expedition under Captain Palliser during the years 1857, 1858, 1859, 1860" map. "Great herds of Buffalo" is written across the area north of the Neutral Hills that would later become Buffalo National Park.

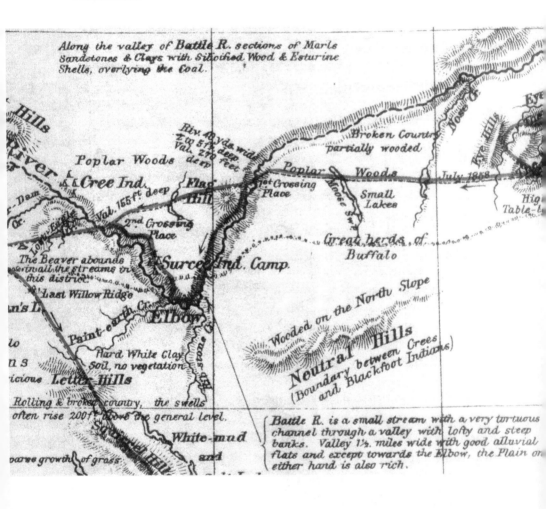

argues that the United States Congress had an unwritten policy that only lands that were considered worthless were set aside as national parks.[41] A similar trend is also noticeable in the establishment of early national parks in Canada, including Buffalo National Park.[42]

Homestead Inspector Joseph Bannerman assumed that the land south and east of the Battle River was not valuable for agriculture as very few had settled in this area.[43] This scanty settlement is apparent on the map titled *Ribstone Creek Sheet* that shows the land disposed of in the park area before 15 October 1907. Although the park was already designated on this map, it clearly shows that much of the land outside the park had yet to be patented.[44] The first superintendent, Edward Ellis, believed no more than 10 per cent of the land in the park was adaptable to farming purposes.[45] Clues about the state of the land in Buffalo National Park played out in the 1912 editorial columns of the *Wainwright Star*[46] in a debate over whether the area would be more profitable if the park area was opened for farming. John Thompson stated that proof of the inferior quality of the land in the area could be seen on a homestead map of the area before its appropriation for the park; it showed that "people were not willing to have [the land as] a gift."[47]

Yet even with the knowledge that the region had historically sustained large herds of bison, it is curious that the land south of Wainwright was even considered for a bison reserve. Originally Elk Island Reserve, now Elk Island National Park, had been earmarked for the bison herd purchased from Michel Pablo. The first two shipments of Pablo bison were in fact transported to Elk Island. However, a letter from Superintendent of Rocky Mountains Park Howard Douglas to Deputy Minister of the Interior William Wallace (W. W.) Cory reveals that it was at Pablo's suggestion that the Dominion government found a new location for the bison effort. Douglas wrote, "In looking over the Elk Park at Lamont Mr. Pablo stated that he did not think it suitable for Buffalo as there was [too] much bush, and the grass is not what the Buffalo are accustomed to. I would strongly recommend that some other location be obtained before the next shipment."[48] Pablo's preference for an area with less bush seems to have been based on his familiarity with the Flathead Valley in Montana. West of the Mission Mountains, Pablo raised his bison in a valley that sported a vegetation primarily of grasses. The Wainwright area, and not Elk Island National Park, seems to resemble more closely a 1908 description of the topography of the Ravalli Hills and Meadows in the Flathead Indian Reservation, an area adjacent to Pablo's bison range: "On the steeper slopes the grazing is

This Department of the Interior map, the Ribstone Creek Sheet, from 15 October 1907 shows the land disposed of in the vicinity of Buffalo National Park. Much of the land on the east side of Buffalo National Park, which had not yet been claimed, has since proved to be the least desirable for agricultural purposes.

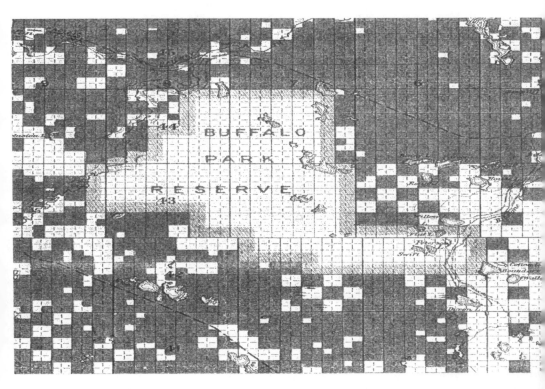

scanty. In the ravines, on the protected slopes, and in the wide heads of gulches, the vegetation is luxuriant."[49]

After Homestead Inspector Joseph Bannerman found a suitable location south of the Battle River, arrangements were made to have an area of approximately 170 square miles set apart for a bison reserve. In 1908, the government spent around $60,000 fencing the park, including a paddock in the northeast corner of the park to display bison for visitors. They needed approximately 70 miles of fence to enclose the area.[50] The first shipment of 325 bison was transferred from Elk Island Park and arrived at the new reserve on 16 June 1909.[51]

While the area north of the Neutral Hills had at one time supported great herds, proponents of the national park little understood the bison's interactions with the land and ecosystem. Before the Europeans arrived, the vast herds of plains bison used enormous territory. As Douglas Bamforth's ecological study of the Great Plains proves, the vegetation's growing seasons and the migration of the bison allowed large herds to subsist on these lands. The plains bison moved according to the availability of grass, which was determined by climate and moisture. However, vegetation was also arranged in a composite, yet mutually dependent, pattern. Bamforth states, "The greater dominance of later-blooming warm-season species in southern [rather] than northern grassland communities also indicates that the bulk of forage production in the south begins later in the year and continues for a shorter period of time than in the north."[52] Although Bamforth studies the Great Plains as a whole, Binnema confirms his theory on a smaller scale in his argument about bison migration in the northern Plains. After wintering in the broad fescue crescent in the northern prairie, the area in which the park was later established, the bison migrated to the moist-mixed prairie in the spring. Although generally dry, this area was wettest in May and June, which allowed protein-rich grasses to tolerate heavy grazing while moisture was present. By July, the blue grama, a protein-rich grass, beckoned the bison to the dry-mixed prairie. In late summer, when the cool weather had slowed the growth of grasses and the range had been depleted, the bison again returned to the moist-mixed prairie where new growth had been encouraged by grazing, summer fires, and falling temperatures. By September, the herds returned to the fescue grassland, found in the parkland, the foothills, or deep river valleys, in preparation for the colder weather and winter storms.[53] Seasonal migration was key to the environment of the Plains, which was intricately arranged to sustain such large herds and at the same time permit the land to recuperate.

Unloading the Pablo bison at the new national park in Wainwright. Photo by J. H. Gano.

Establishing Buffalo National Park was a means for the Dominion government to use non-arable land while at the same time restoring bison to the modern Canadian West. Those administering the bison effort at Buffalo National Park would soon realize that this task would be more difficult than first imagined. While reports of early explorers had shown the Wainwright area had been productive as a bison range in the past, with the onset of settlement, how the land north of the Neutral Hills could be used had changed. The necessity for a fence around the park created a closed ecosystem, which did not take into consideration the most important characteristic of the bison species—its migratory nature. Those involved in planning the park did not understand the intricacies and fragility of the parkland environment and how bison interacted with this environment.

The ignorance about the importance of interactions between bison and their environment (the flora, landscape, and predators) shows the limitations of the wildlife science in the early 20th century. While it would have been impossible to establish a park on the Prairies that accommodated traditional bison migration patterns, an understanding of this facet of bison ecology could have restrained park officials from allowing the herd to grow so quickly. Shortly after the effort began, the rapidly increasing bison herd proved too much for the resource base in the area to bear.

Notes

1.   John Warkentin, ed., *The Western Interior of Canada: A Record of Geographical Discovery 1612 to 1917* (Toronto 1964), 147.

2.   Library and Archives Canada, Ottawa, ON (hereafter LAC), Certified Copy of a Report of the Committee of the Privy Council, approved by His Excellency the Governor General on the 7 March 1908, Parks Canada Files, BNP, RG 84, Vol. 982, File BU2[548608], pt. 2.

3.   LAC, Minister of the Interior to F. T. Griffin, 7 Aug. 1907, J. W. Greenway to J. B. Harkin, n.d., and J. A. Bannerman to Frank Oliver, 20 Aug. 1907, Parks Canada Files, Buffalo National Park [BNP], RG 84, Vol. 981, File BU2[548608], pt. 1.

4.   Irene Spry, Introduction, in John Palliser, *The Papers of the Palliser Expedition, 1857–1860,* (Toronto 1968), xv, xxii–xxiii; John Palliser, *The Papers of the Palliser Expedition, 1857–1860,* (Toronto 1968), 1; W. L. Morton, *Henry Youle Hind, 1823–1908* (Toronto 1980), 30, 58.

5.   Hind's report was published three years before Palliser's report was released. Also commissioned to draw the maps for the Palliser expedition, John Arrowsmith had access to Palliser's data; thus, some of this information was incorporated into Hind's map even before the data were published in Palliser's *Further Papers*. John Warkentin, "Steppe, Desert and Empire," in A.W. Rasporich and H.C. Klassen eds. *Prairie Perspectives 2* (Toronto 1973), 118–19.

6.   Palliser, *Papers*, 9, 18–20.

7.   Palliser, *Papers*, 16.

8.   Henry Youle Hind, *British North America: Reports of Progress Together with a Preliminary and General Report on the Assiniboine and Saskatchewan Exploring Expedition* (London 1860).

9.   John Palliser, James Hector, and J.W. Sullivan, "Progress of the British North American Exploring Expedition," *Journal of the Royal Geographical Society of London* 30 (1860), 286.

10. Irene Spry writes that the border between the true prairie and fertile belt on the 1859 map was "an irregular curve running northwest across the South Saskatchewan, upstream from modern Saskatoon, to near modern Unity and thence westward, south of Battle River, and across the Red Deer, swinging to the south again a few miles east of today's No. 2 Highway from Edmonton to Calgary." Spry, Introduction, *Papers*, cviii.

11. William Francis Butler, *The Great Lone Land: A Narrative of Travel and Adventure in the North-West of America* (Edmonton 1968), 230.

12. *North West of Canada: A General Sketch of the Extent, Woods and Forests, Mineral Resources and Climatology of the Four Provisional Districts of Assiniboia, Saskatchewan, Alberta and Athabasca* (Ottawa 1887), 5–6.

13. Warkentin, "Steppe, Desert and Empire," 127; Doug Owram, *Promise of Eden: The Canadian Expansionist Movement and the Idea of the West, 1856–1900* (Toronto 1980), 150.

14. Palliser, *Papers*, 138.

15. John Macoun, *Manitoba and the Great North-West: The Field for Investment; The Home of the Emigrant* (London 1883), 57–59, 76, 171.

16. Dominion land surveyors mapped out the North West into one-square-mile sections. A township is thirty-six sections together in a six-mile by six-mile block.

17. Provincial Archives of Alberta, Edmonton, AB (hereafter PAA), Tom Kains, Diary, 1883, Dominion Land Surveyor Records, File 79.27, Box 2825.

18. PAA, James Garden, Field Notes of Block Survey West of the Fourth Initial Meridian, (hereafter Field Notes), North-West Territories, Surveyed by James Garden, 21 Jul.–22 Aug. 1884, Dominion Land Surveyor Records, File 83.376, Box 904.

19. PAA, James Garden, Field Notes, 27 Jun.–19 Jul. 1884, Dominion Land Surveyor Records, File 83.376, Box 903. In fact, Garden's field notes record rolling sand ridges just east of the Ribstone Creek, on section 36 of township 42, range 6.

20. PAA, James Garden, Field Notes, 21 Jul.–22 Aug. 1884, Dominion Land Surveyor Records, File 83.376, Box 904.

21. PAA, James Garden, Field Notes, 27 Jun.–19 Jul. 1884, Dominion Land Surveyor Records, File 83.376, Box 903.

22. PAA, C. C. Fairchild, Field Notes of Township 42, Range 5, West of the 4th Mer., Surveyed by C. C. Fairchild, 1–17 Sept. 1903, Dominion Land Surveyor Records, File 83.376, Box 1776a.

23. PAA, M. B. Weekes, Field Notes of Township 44, Range 8, West of the 4th Mer., Surveyed by M. B. Weekes, 18 Sept.–17 Oct. 1903, Dominion Land Surveyor Records, File 83.376, Box 1910.

24. Warkentin, "Steppe, Desert and Empire," 106.

25. Anthony Hendry, *The Journal of Anthony Hendry, 1754–55: York Factory to the Blackfeet Country*, Lawrence J. Burpee ed. (Toronto 1973), 26, 27.

26. Palliser, *Papers*, 243.

27. Theodore Binnema, *Common and Contested Ground: A Human and Environmental History of the Northwestern Plains* (Norman 2001), 39.

28. Binnema, *Common and Contested Ground*, 40, 45, 47–48.

29. J. Roderick Vickers, *Alberta Plains Prehistory: A Review* (Edmonton 1986), 7–8.

30. George W. Arthur, *An Introduction to the Ecology of the Early Historic Communal Bison Hunting Among the Northern Plains Indians* (Ottawa 1975), 106.

31. Arthur, *Introduction to the Ecology of Bison Hunting*, 13–16.

32. Irene Spry, "The Great Transformation: The Disappearance of the Commons in Western Canada," in Richard Allen ed. *Man and Nature on the Prairies* (Regina 1976), 21.

33. Palliser, *Papers*, 242.

34. *Transactions of the Ethnological Society of London,* vol. 1 (London 1861), 249. While the Neutral Hills were believed to be a boundary, it is clear that such borders were not inflexible. Jack Brink, in *Dog Days in Southern Alberta* (Edmonton 1986), 56, has argued that the Blackfoot territory went as far north as the valley of the North Saskatchewan River. In fact, Palliser encountered a Blackfoot medicine lodge southwest of the park, two miles on the east side of the Battle River near Hardisty, Alberta. Palliser, *Papers*, 244.

35. Paul S. Martin and Christine R. Szuter, "War Zones and Game Sinks in Lewis and Clark's West," *Conservation Biology* 13 (February 1999), 38, 42–44.

36. Martin and Szuter, "War Zones and Game Sinks," 43.

37. For example, see *The Journals, Detailed Reports, and Observations Relative to the Exploration, by Captain Palliser, of that Portion of British North America, which, in Latitude, Lies Between the British Boundary Line and the Height of Land of Watershed of the Northern or Frozen Ocean Respectively, and in Longitude, Between the Western Shore of Lake Superior and the Pacific Ocean During the Years 1857, 1858, 1859, and 1860* (London 1863), 52, 53, 55.

38. *Journals, Detailed Reports, and Observations,* 52.

39. *Journals, Detailed Reports, and Observations,* 53.

40. See "A General Map of the Routes in British North America Explored by the Expedition Under Captain Palliser During the years 1857, 1858, 1859, 1860," in Palliser, *Papers.*

41. Alfred Runte, *National Parks: The American Experience* (Lincoln 1979), 49.

42. Robert Craig Brown, "The Doctrine of Usefulness: Natural Resource and National Park Policy in Canada, 1887–1914," in J. G. Nelson ed. *Canadian Parks in Perspective* (Montreal 1969), 48–49.

43. LAC, Memorandum to W. W. Cory, 6 Apr. 1918, Parks Canada Files, BNP, RG 84, Vol. 982, File BU2[548608], pt. 2.

44. *Ribstone Creek Sheet*, 15 Oct. 1907, Map Collection, G3471, G4, s380, 266, Glenbow Archives, Calgary, AB. A patent was the right or title to an area of land granted by the Dominion government.

45. LAC, Edward Ellis to J. B. Harkin, 4 May 1912, Parks Canada Files, BNP, RG 84, Vol. 982, File BU2[548608], pt. 2.

46. See, for example, *Wainwright Star*, 20 Dec. 1912, John Thompson, "Farmer Argues That Buffalo Is Bird in Hand"; *Wainwright Star*, Dec. 1912, "'Are Rural Residents to Suffer for This Paltry Tourist Trade?' He Asks," and others, LAC, Parks Canada Files, BNP, RG 84, Vol. 982, File BU2[548608], pt, 2.

47. *Wainwright Star*, 20 Dec. 1912, John Thompson, "Farmer Argues That Buffalo Is Bird in Hand," LAC, Parks Canada Files, BNP, RG 84, Vol. 982, File BU2[548608], pt, 2.

48. LAC, Howard Douglas to W. W. Cory, 11 Jun. 1907, Parks Canada Files, BNP, RG 84, Vol. 51, File BU209, pt. 1.

49. Morton J. Elrod, "The Flathead Buffalo Range," in *Annual Report of the American Bison Society, 1905–1907* (n.p.: American Bison Society, 1908), 29.

50. LAC, Minister of the Interior to F. T. Griffin, 7 Aug. 1907, J. W. Greenway to J. B. Harkin, n.d., and R. H. Campbell to C.U. Ryley, 21 Sept. 1908, Parks Canada Files, Buffalo National Park [hereafter BNP], RG 84, Vol. 981, File BU2[548608], pt. 1; LAC, Certified Copy of a Report of the Committee of the Privy Council, approved by His Excellency the Governor General on the 7th March 1908, Parks Canada Files, BNP, RG 84, Vol. 982, File BU2[548608], pt. 2; LAC, Mr. Courtice to J. B. Harkin, 13 Nov. 1916, Parks Canada Files, BNP, RG 84, Vol. 53, File[BU232], pt. 1.

51. LAC, A. G. Smith, "Statement of Original Shipments of Buffalo into Buffalo Park, Wainwright," 14 Sep. 1926, Parks Canada Files, BNP, RG 84, Vol. 51, File BU209, pt. 3.

52. Douglas B. Bamforth, *Ecology and Human Organization on the Great Plains* (New York 1988), 65.

53. Binnema, *Common and Contested Ground*, 40–43, 45, 47.

CHAPTER TWO

Bison Conservation and Buffalo National Park

1908–1920

ALL EARLY NATIONAL PARK POLICIES WERE INFLUENCED by the experience of Canada's first national park, Rocky Mountains Park (now Banff National Park). As this park was established during the heyday of the Conservation Movement, its development was influenced by the utilitarian spirit of this movement and its motives of control and exploitation to benefit the nation. Rocky Mountains Park was founded in 1887 in order to profit from the discovery of the Banff Hot Springs; all ensuing policies governing this park during this early period were driven by economic motives, with an emphasis on commercialism and the development of resources. Despite these motives, however, the *Rocky Mountains Park Act* of 1887 still laid the foundation for a preservationist policy for national parks in general, and specifically for game animals.[1] Historian Sid Marty argues that "Canadian legislators tried to frame an act that would make the reserve a commercial success, but save it from the abuses of the ignorant and the avaricious."[2]

When Buffalo Park Reserve, later to become Buffalo National Park, was established in 1908, the national park system in Canada was only two decades old. The experience of this park, however, seems at first to be a departure from the commercial motives inherent in the establishment of the other early mountain parks. As a prairie park, Buffalo National Park had little to offer in terms of exploitable resources or commercial potential. Whereas game in the mountain parks was preserved and propagated because it brought revenue to the park, the Dominion government's purchase of the Pablo bison herd was devoid of profit-making motives.

Those administrating the effort at Buffalo National Park, first the Department of the Interior and then, in 1911, the Parks Branch, did not intend to profit from the bison. However, they did not foresee the management problems and expense that accompanied the rapid growth of the herd. Within the first decade, the Dominion government had the largest bison herd in the world and the Parks Branch was forced to rethink the management of the herd and the direction of the effort. They quickly realized that the bison could not be saved on sentiment alone. Just like the game in the mountain national parks, the Parks Branch needed to make the bison profitable to sustain the effort at Buffalo National Park.

In 1885, the Banff mineral hot springs were discovered by two prospectors and a Canadian Pacific Railway employee. In the spirit of progress and development that dominated this period, the Dominion government annexed the area before these individuals could lay any private claims.[3] The Dominion government knew that such natural wonders were profitable. Prime Minister John A. Macdonald boasted:

> They are the only hot springs so far as I know yet discovered in the Dominion and their value in my opinion can scarcely be estimated and should not be allowed to go into the hands of a private speculator but should be owned by the government as a National Sanitarium in the same way as the hot springs of Arkansas are...for the United States.[4]

Similar policies drove the establishment of other national parks along the Canadian Pacific Railway line. Glacier and Yoho reserves were set aside the following year to make the railway through the mountains in British Columbia more popular and profitable.[5]

Given that the early national parks in Canada were established during, and influenced by, the Conservation Movement, it is not surprising that a more utilitarian approach is apparent in their development and in the safeguarding of resources in them for the Dominion. The movement began in the United States in the 1860s, when individuals, prompted by the near obliteration of natural resources through exploitive measures, called for efforts to ensure that resources be available for future generations. Advocates like painter George Catlin, ornithologist and painter John James Audubon, and writer Henry David Thoreau, started to lobby for the preservation of wilderness. The beginning of the movement is marked by the publication of George Perkins Marsh's book *Man and Nature* (1864), which prompted North Americans to rethink society's relationship with the natural environment.[6]

The Canadian movement, which began in the late 19th century and continued until the early 1920s, started in the forestry sector in Ontario and Quebec, where it was realized that sustainability of the industry hinged on careful management of natural resources. The movement started to solidify when lumbermen from Quebec and members of the Ontario Fruit Growers' Association, who were concerned with the how deforestation had affected the agrarian environment, were invited to attended the inaugural meeting of the American Forestry Congress in Cincinnati, Ohio, in April 1882. At this congress, a second meeting of the association was planned for Montreal in August of the same year, an event that historians Peter Gillis and Thomas Roach mark as the beginning of the Conservation Movement in Canada.[7]

In the American Conservation Movement, two different schools of thought emerged. A more preservationist school, whose followers advocated that nature should be safeguarded from development and left unaltered, was led by writer and nature enthusiast John Muir (1838–1914).[8] Gifford Pinchot and other professional foresters, however, believed wise use, efficiency, and rational planning could ensure the permanence of resources in the future.[9] In Canada, the Conservation Movement followed this latter, more conservationist, stance. One reason for this was that the movement was led by scientific farmers and lumbermen. In fact, Canadian civil servants looked to American forest industry trends to help define their conservation policies. In particular, Gifford Pinchot, chief forester in the Roosevelt government, provided advice to Canadian government officials, such as Minister of the Interior Clifford Sifton and Superintendent of Forestry Elihu Stewart, based on economic arguments and trends in scientific forestry and land management in the United States.[10] Furthermore, the "myth of superabundance," the belief that the natural wealth of the country was inexhaustible, was much more prevalent in Canada given that the country had a larger wilderness area than that of the United States and a much smaller population.[11]

The Conservation Movement was certainly influential in the establishment of the early Canadian national parks. In his theory, the "doctrine-of-usefulness," historian Robert Craig Brown argues early national park policy was "a continuation of the general resource policy that grew out of the National Policy of the [John A.] Macdonald government. Underlying parks policy was the assumption of the existence of plentiful natural resources within the reserves capable of exploitation and the principle of shared responsibility of government and private enterprise in the development of those resources."[12] Control and exploitation of natural resources, however, were not in conflict with the development of national parks. Rather, the two concepts were tied closely together.[13]

While motives of control and profit were driving forces in the establishment of the early mountain parks, it would be wrong to assume that early national park philosophy had no preservationist ideals. The 1887 *Rocky Mountains Park Act*, which officially created Rocky Mountains Park (now Banff National Park), addressed the general preservation and protection of game, fish, and birds.[14] The seemingly antagonistic concepts of preservation and development brought the whole area into usefulness. Thus, although the hot springs were initially the "most easily exploitable asset,"[15] other resources of the Rocky Mountains reserve were also considered valuable. Mineral deposits and timber were jewels that if harvested would profit the Dominion crown.[16] Even scenery became a valuable commodity, indispensable to creating tourist demand. J. B. Harkin, Commissioner of Dominion Parks from 1911–1936, calculated that the mountain scenery was worth $13.88 an acre, much more than the wheat-producing Prairies, which were valued at only $4.91 an acre.[17]

Historian Alan MacEachern notes that politicians who created Rocky Mountains Park were not only interested in profiting from the area's resources, but were also concerned with protecting timber and other resources that were aesthetically valuable to the park. Furthermore, setting aside areas for parks placed restrictions on how the land and resources could be used.[18] Sid Marty argues that the Canadian national park system, although influenced by the example set by the United States, was more functionally preservationist. While Yellowstone National Park's was established to protect that wilderness area, in reality it suffered neglect for fourteen years. In fact, the United States Army had to take control of the area in 1886 to halt destruction of the land and wild animals.[19]

It is interesting that the value of game was recognized almost immediately after the establishment of Rocky Mountains Park, given that it was initially overlooked in the Canadian Conservation Movement, which was more concerned with forestry and other natural resources.[20] In fact, wild animals were not even overtly acknowledged until around 1917, when Clifford Sifton in the *Review of the Work of the Commission of Conservation* introduced the new branch devoted to conserving animal populations as an "unusual interest."[21] The term "wildlife," in fact, was not even used in the first part of the 20th century.[22] This neglect is no doubt related to the close connection between conservation and economic utility and the difficulty in making the argument for game preservation based on utility. While there are isolated examples of conservation measures, for example, the 1894 *Unorganized Territories Game Protection Act* passed to protect the wood bison and other game as a food supply for the local native populations,[23] on the whole it seems that initially the Dominion government did not consider wild animals to have the same value as other resources.[24]

In North America, sportsmen, interested in preserving their own recreational opportunities, were some of the early advocates for the welfare of game. In the United States, the Boone and Crockett Club, founded by Theodore Roosevelt in 1887, was a means for sportsmen to preserve big game populations that were rapidly being depleted by overhunting. In fact, hunters, concerned to preserve animal populations for sport, became involved in ensuring Yellowstone National Park remained a refuge for big game.[25] Similarly, the near annihilation of the plains bison motivated American sportsmen to make protection of wild animals a public issue.[26]

In Canada, concern for game arose among regional and local organizations in the central and eastern provinces. Having witnessed the destruction of their populations, natural history societies and fish-and-game clubs successfully lobbied their respective provincial governments to take responsibility for game resources as early as the 1890s for both aesthetic and recreational reasons.[27] George Altmeyer points out that while the Conservation Movement in Canada had a pragmatic side, it also had a moral and aesthetic dimension—a philosophy of "unselfishness." One event that accelerated the wildlife Conservation Movement was the near extinction of the plains bison.[28]

Even before its establishment of Rocky Mountains Park, the Minister of the Interior asked former Commissioner of Fisheries W. F. Whitcher to examine the proposed park area and make recommendations for the protection of wild animals, birds, and fish. Whitcher recommended strict control of hunting and fishing to help increase the species that had been depleted by hunting during the railway construction. His recommendation was incorporated into the *Rocky Mountains Park Act*.[29] Unfortunately, protection of various species was nearly impossible to regulate until 1909 when the first year-round warden service was implemented.[30]

While the *Rocky Mountains Park Act* was one of the earliest moves to protect and preserve game in the federal jurisdiction, proponents of this preservation in the early national parks shared the motives of the regional and local advocates. Game was a commodity: it was protected to ensure its availability for aesthetic and recreational purposes and to enhance scenery inside the park and sport outside. Ultimately, everyone connected with Rocky Mountains Park (the railway, the federal government, the park, and the businesses inside the park) had vested interests in game both from its conservation inside the park and its depletion outside park borders.[31]

Wild animals in Rocky Mountains Park and the other mountain parks quickly became one of the most valuable resources. During his administration (1897–1912), Park Superintendent Howard Douglas strengthened the park's conservationist stance and implemented more stringent regulations to protect game.[32] Not only did he increase the indigenous animal populations during his administration, but he also established the first park zoo in 1907 to draw tourists.[33] Douglas's enthusiasm for the growing animal populations in Rocky Mountains Park can be seen in his annual reports, wherein he took every opportunity to "draw the Minister's attention to the increasing wildlife numbers within the park, particularly the buffalo, which were reproducing steadily, and to emphasize their growing importance as a tourist attraction."[34] This emphasis on animals as an economic asset was necessary: "Douglas knew… that the way to win [government] support was to demonstrate that both parks and wildlife were valuable attractions, that policies for their care and protection could become commercially viable propositions."[35] By 1906, Douglas had achieved this goal: "Wildlife was accounting for much of the park's growing popularity and thus paying for itself many times over."[36]

While the mountain parks were able to profit from their scenery and natural resources, the first two prairie parks, Elk Island Reserve, established in 1906, and Buffalo Park Reserve, established in 1908, could not be commercially exploited in the same way. There were no resources considered of value in these parks when they were established. The Beaver Hills area was continually ravaged by fire in the 1890s, which destroyed much of the timber and severely damaged the landscape. The destruction of this region by fire was the main reason that Cooking Lake Forest Reserve, a 170 square mile area in the Beaver Hills locality, was established. A portion of this reserve was later set aside as Elk Island Reserve (1899).[37]

The land south of Wainwright was appropriated for Buffalo Park Reserve because the area was considered undesirable for agriculture. In fact, the act of using this land as a sanctuary for the plains bison was initially the sole exploitive action; there were no known resources in the area when the park was established. Even though the Wainwright area later proved to be rich in oil and gas, development of these resources did not begin in the region until the 1920s and they were never tapped while the area was under park jurisdiction.[38]

Furthermore, the scenery of Buffalo National Park did not have the same potential to lure tourist dollars as did the mountain parks. The sandy, dune-covered parkland simply could not compete with the sublime land-scape of the Rocky Mountains. Buffalo Park Reserve's recreational area, Mott Lake, opened as a resort in the northern part of the park in 1917. This "much celebrated picnic spot with booths, change houses, swings, and a sandy beach patrolled by a lifeguard,"[39] however, could hardly compete with the recreational opportunities available in the mountains. Moreover, although the park was on the Grand Trunk Pacific line, it was not close to a larger centre. Consequently, it is unlikely that the government established the park with motives to exploit or even control the resources within.

Rather, it appears that these first two prairie parks were established for the purpose of preserving endangered species, a departure from the resource exploitation inherent in the establishment of the mountain parks. Elk Island Reserve was founded because of a genuine concern for the elk in the area, which, before 1906, were threatened by hunters and wild fires. Local citizens took the initiative. W. H. Cooper, a North-West Territories game warden from Edmonton, informed the local member of Parliament, Frank Oliver, of the peril the elk in the area faced unless measures were taken to protect them. After local residents lobbied the government, Clifford Sifton, Minister of the Interior, set aside a portion of Cooking Lake Forest Reserve as a wildlife sanctuary.[40]

From the moment the Dominion government had the opportunity to pur-chase the last and largest free-ranging herd on the continent, it was clear that the plains bison were viewed very differently from other wild animals because the species was threatened with extinction. Wanton hunting and the encroach-ment of settlement in the West caused the virtual disappearance of the plains bison on the Canadian Plains.[41] In the United States, they existed only in small pockets. Their uncertain fate made the species iconic.[42] In the United States, the plains bison became equated with the disappearance of the "Wild West." It was believed that if bison were not saved from extinction, other icons and symbols of American culture would also disappear.[43] In Canada, the tone was more muted, but the sentiment was unmistakeably similar. According to I. S. MacLaren, the bison operated as a symbol of western wildness. To early Euro-peans, the animal came to represent the Canadian West itself: "the buffalo acts synecdochically: the buffalo *is* the prairie."[44] C. Gordon Hewitt, writing in the 1920s, noted that "[t]he history of the buffalo in North America con-stitutes one of the greatest tragedies in animal life in historical times."[45] These popular and nostalgic sentiments would play an influential role in the estab-lishment and management of Buffalo National Park.

The near extinction of the plains bison also signalled the fate that might await other wild animals.[46] The disappearance of game populations in the United States with the onset of settlement was enough to evoke the fear of a similar trend in Canada. Janet Foster writes that North-West Mounted Police (NWMP) started to record rapidly declining game populations in the Canadian West in the 1880s. The NWMP were concerned not only because animal species were in danger of becoming extinct, but also because the disappearance of game would result in the elimination of a food source that was vital to the survival of many Native populations.[47] Thus bison symbolized more than the disappearance of a bygone era. They were a vivid reminder of humanity's destructive and greedy character.

The purchase of the Pablo bison by the Dominion government and the creation of Buffalo Park Reserve was also a departure from the motives of control and exploitation inherent in the founding of the early mountain parks. The plains bison's near-extinct status and their symbolic importance to the region may have motivated the purchase of the Pablo herd. By the time of the purchase, wild plains bison had been absent from the Canadian Plains for almost two decades. Although most of the remaining bison in the United States were in private herds, contemporaries considered the Pablo herd to be the last free-ranging plains bison herd on the continent. These animals represented a link not only to the region's past, but also to the Canadian West as a whole.

Civil servants in the Dominion government have been credited with the forethought given to saving the species.[48] Alex Ayotte, a Canadian Land Agent working in Montana, was the first to see the potential opportunity of the purchase of the Pablo bison herd. The United States government had applied the *Dawes Act* in the Flathead Valley, and the reservation where Pablo grazed his bison was being thrown open for settlement.[49] J. Obed Smith, Commissioner of Immigration, forwarded Ayotte's suggestion to W. W. Scott, Superintendent of Immigration in Ottawa, in late 1905. It stated that Michel Pablo was "anxious to move his herd of buffalo, consisting of 360 head, from Montana to Western Canada." and suggested that the government might want to acquire more bison for Banff National Park.[50] Initially, W. W. Cory, the deputy minister, turned down the proposal, likely because he had been informed that Howard Douglas believed the Banff herd was as large as that park could accommodate.[51]

The Dominion government, however, quickly changed its mind, evidence that competition for the herd was one of the stronger motives driving the purchase. In March 1906, Benjamin Davies, another Canadian Land Agent in Great Falls, Montana, reiterated Pablo's plea for a location in Western Canada on which to graze his bison herd. Pablo was also open to selling the bison to the Canadian government for a reasonable price. Despite some government resistance, Douglas fought for the acquisition of the herd. Eleanor Luxton, a former resident of Banff, stated in an interview that when Frank Oliver, Minister of the Interior, delayed making a decision for six months, Douglas carried on "quite a fight to get the buffalo purchase through."[52] Sid Marty notes that it was only after Douglas sent Deputy Minister W. W. Cory a newspaper clipping revealing the plans of the American Bison Society to buy up the private herds of plains bison in the United States that he received word to close the deal.[53] By the end of March, W. W. Cory was inquiring after details of Pablo's asking price and by June, Howard Douglas, later to be one of the main movers in this bison preservation effort, had gone to Montana to inspect the bison herd.[54]

Rivalry is also apparent in the government's efforts to acquire all of Pablo's bison when it was found that the herd was larger than originally thought.[55] Clearly the cost was secondary to purchasing the bison before the Americans could. When there was news that some Americans were attempting to offer Pablo more money for his bison, Douglas showed the Dominion government's contract called for the entire herd less the ten heifer calves and two bulls Pablo wanted for himself.[56] The Dominion government did not need more bison to save the species. Rather, as Douglas confirms, the government was more interested in spiting those in the United States who wanted the herd: "as our contract calls for the whole herd, I think we should take every hoof. If you knew the amount of bluff the Americans are putting up you would feel like giving them a lesson."[57]

The purchase of the Pablo bison herd was also an opportunity for the Dominion government to advertise Canada in line with the spirit of boosterism that marked this era—when conservation of game populations promoted the idea that Canada was a wealthy nation with a superabundance of resources.[58] Howard Douglas stated that, with the purchase of the herd, "Canada would own 8/10 of all the Buffalo living" which would be a "great advertisement for Canada."[59] He believed the herd to be very cheap, and he anticipated "a great howl from the Americans should the [Dominion] Government decide to purchase them."[60]

Keeping the negotiations for the herd's purchase secret became more urgent when the American Bison Society made known its intention, in

January 1907, to purchase all the remaining bison in the United States and Canada and present them to the United States government.[61] The Dominion government also became anxious to sign the deal with Pablo when details of the sale of his bison to the Canadians were prematurely leaked to the *Great Falls Daily Tribune* by Billy Gird. Gird, it was reported, was a "cow puncher" who claimed "he was sent on official business by the Canadian Government to inspect the herd and tally them."[62] Even though Pablo had signed an agreement with the Dominion government by March 1907, there was fear that the United States might step in and prevent the transfer.[63]

The Dominion government was very willing to spend extra money on the effort, proof that the profit motive was not driving the purchase. The decision to move the bison to a new park south of Wainwright could not have been economically beneficial, especially when Elk Island Reserve lay much closer to Edmonton and had greater tourism potential. Establishing a new park was a substantial investment because the reserve needed to be fenced and the area prepared for the bison. Extra money was spent to transport the first two shipments from Elk Island to the new park. The third shipment from Montana—the first to go directly to the Wainwright park— also proved costly. The Grand Trunk Railway had not yet been completed west of Wainwright because the Battle River Trestle was still under construction. Instead, Howard Douglas decided to ship the bison via Regina and Saskatoon to arrive at the park from the east on the Grand Trunk Pacific line.[64] This decision cost more because the distance was "some four or five hundred miles further than would otherwise be necessary" and the Department of the Interior needed to pay the balance of freight charges and wages for Pablo's men that exceeded the initial agreement.[65] When it became apparent that capturing and moving the bison from the Flathead Valley, Montana, to Alberta would take much longer and cost more than anticipated, Parliament approved an extra $75,000 on top of the original funding of $100,000.[66]

The Dominion government continued to purchase as many of Pablo's bison as it could until 1912, when the contract was officially closed. Even then, the Parks Branch informed him that it was still open to news of further shipments.[67] Thirty bison were also purchased from the C. E. Conrad Estate in Kalispell, Montana,[68] and some were transferred to Buffalo National Park from Rocky Mountains Park (see Table 1).[69]

TABLE I: PURCHASE DATES AND SHIPMENT LOCATIONS		
Date	*Shipment Location*	*Number of Bison*
16 June 1909	transferred from Elk Island Park	325
3 July 1909	3rd shipment from Montana	190
17 October 1909	4th shipment from Montana	28
31 October 1909	transferred from Banff	77
12 June 1910	5th shipment from Montana	46
17 October 1910	6th shipment from Montana	28
23 November 1910	1st shipment from Conrad Herd	15
20 April 1911	2nd shipment from Conrad Herd	15
30 May 1911	7th shipment from Montana	7
30 June 1912	8th shipment from Montana	7
31 March 1914	transferred from Banff	10
	Total	748

Source: LAC, A. G. Smith, "Statement of Original Shipments of Buffalo into Buffalo Park, Wainwright," 14 Sept. 1926, Parks Canada Files, Buffalo National Park, RG 84, Vol. 51, File BU209, pt. 3. On the dates Oct. 31, 1909 and Mar. 31, 1914, the original document reads "Transferred ex. Banff," which suggests bison were exchanged with Buffalo National Park on these two dates.

Although competitive motives drove the purchase of the Pablo herd, the Dominion government showed some preservationist ethic. Douglas ensured the bison were healthy. For example, for one of the early shipments he reported to W. W. Cory, Deputy Minister of the Interior, a herd of about 220 head was said to have been inspected by a veterinarian who "found them all in good Condition and free from any disease."[70] When Michel Pablo raised concerns about the suitability of Elk Island Reserve as a sanctuary for bison,[71] the government took his advice and immediately made efforts to secure a new location south of Wainwright. This new reserve, Buffalo Park Reserve in 1908, would become Buffalo National Park in 1913.[72]

In the early years of the effort, there was no clear policy for managing the bison herd. The bison-saving effort was treading in new territory. At the time the Pablo bison herd was purchased, there was little knowledge of, or precedent for, effective means to save and propagate wild animals other than in the mountain parks. Not until the 1930s did the study of relationships of species with each other and their environment and ideas such as carrying capacity, what we today call wildlife science, start to surface among park and wildlife managers.[73] The growth of the bison herd population, however, appears to have been one indicator of the saving effort's success. When Howard Douglas first viewed the Pablo bison in Montana, he seemed pleased to find that the herd had increased with little attention. He estimated the herd numbered 350 and believed "there should be 1000 head in five years with ordinary good luck."[74] The nucleus herd of 748 bison imported into the park increased very rapidly. In 1916, four years after the final shipment of the Pablo bison, the herd at Wainwright already exceeded 2,000 head. Newspaper headlines began to boast that Canada now had the largest bison herd in the world.[75] Gordon Hewitt, the Dominion entomologist and consulting zoologist, was pleased with the successful growth of the herd:

> Under these eminently natural conditions the buffalo have increased annually. In the spring of 1913 the numbers had increased to 1,188 head; a year later there were 1,453 buffalo. When I visited the buffalo park in 1915 there were over 2,000 buffalo. In June, 1919, the herd had increased to 3,830 animals. In other words, there are at the present time in the Buffalo Park at Wainwright, Alta., under the care and protection of the Canadian Government, more buffalo than existed on the whole North American continent eight years ago, and by far the largest herd of buffalo in existence.[76]

While Hewitt was impressed with the Dominion government's role in bringing back the bison, he also raised concern over what was to be done with surplus. In an earlier article he wrote, "In the Buffalo Park at Wainwright, Alberta, this question is becoming a serious one as they will soon occupy as much range as is capable of sustaining them."[77] As early as 1916, the Parks Branch showed concerned about the cost of maintaining the rapidly increasing bison herd. J. B. Harkin, commissioner of National Parks, feared that

> [w]hile the maintenance of this herd for the time being I believe has the full backing of public opinion this condition may [not] always continue. At present the backing is the result of sentiment alone. This sentiment arises out of a natural desire to preserve specimens of the original dominant animal of the plains and I think is accentuated by a national pride with respect to the coup which resulted in the transfer of the Pablo herd from the United States to Canada. Sooner or later, however, as time goes on I anticipate an increasing number of people will question why a considerable amount of money should be spent annually upon the preservation of the buffalo.[78]

The same concern was emphasized in a letter to Maxwell Graham, Chief of Park Animals, likely also written by Harkin: "sooner or later sentiment alone will not be sufficient to hold public opinion with us in the matter of very large expenditures upon the buffalo here when the people of the country are not getting any clearly tangible benefit therefrom."[79] His suggestion that the cattalo experiments, which were moved to Buffalo National Park in 1916, would "help in this connection" shows the department was beginning to search for ways to make the bison herd useful.[80] Clearly the thinking of the Parks Branch had shifted to more a more conservationist stance, when, in 1920, Harkin expressed, "We naturally want to dispose of them to the best advantage for the country, and the heads and hides of course have a definite value."[81]

Initially the bison-preservation effort at Buffalo National Park stood as a departure from the exploitive management applied to the game in the mountain parks. The rapid increase of the herd in the first decade and the accompanying expense forced the Parks Branch to make an about-face, however. This is perhaps best illustrated by the offer the department received to purchase the Scotty Phillips bison herd from South Dakota. When they were first considering the offer of 430 bison in 1914, the same competitive spirit which drove the

Pablo purchase is unmistakable in their reasoning: "the Dominion acquiring the last large herd of good buffalo left in the United States [would] thus not only [improve] its own herd, but [leave] the United States that much the poorer."[82] Yet, they did not purchase the herd, and in 1920 it was still available. This time, however, it is clear that J. B. Harkin was no longer swayed by such competitive or sentimental justifications. He wrote, "We now have the dominating buffalo herd of the world and I scarcely think our aim should be to have *all* the buffalo in the world. Our own herds are increasing so rapidly that we are perilously near our range limitations."[83]

As was proved by the time the Park's first decade ended, the bison-saving effort at Buffalo National Park could not survive on sentiment and aesthetics alone. While the purchase of the Pablo herd and the establishment of Buffalo National Park had not been driven by a concern for profit initially, as the expense of the effort increased, the Parks Branch began to explore ways to exploit the only resource of value in the park—the bison. With no other form of revenue, the department began to consider a more conservationist management method, similar to the policies applied to the game populations in the mountain parks. This decision, however, opened the door for the government to pursue even greater exploitive measures to profit from its new-found resource.

Notes

1. Foster, *Working for Wildlife*, 26.

2. Sid Marty, *A Grand and Fabulous Notion: The First Century of Canada's Parks* (Toronto 1984), 64.

3. Foster, *Working for Wildlife*, 19.

4. Foster, *Working for Wildlife*, 18–19.

5. Kevin McNamee, "From Wild Places to Endangered Spaces: A History of Canada's National Parks," in Philip Dearden and Rick Rollins, eds., *Parks and Protected Areas in Canada: Planning and Management* (Toronto 1993), 21.

6. Peter Gillis and Thomas R. Roach, "The Beginnings of a Movement: The Montreal Congress and Its Aftermath, 1880–1896," in Chad Gaffield and Pam Gaffield, eds., *Consuming Canada: Readings in Environmental History* (Toronto 1995), 131; Roderick Frazier Nash, *Wilderness and the American Mind*, 4th ed. (New Haven 2001), 104–105.

7. Gillis and Roach, "Beginnings of a Movement," 131–132, 135, 140, 148.

8. Nash, *Wilderness*, 122.

9. Samuel P. Hays, *Conservation and the Gospel of Efficiency: The Progressive Conservation Movement, 1890–1920* (Cambridge 1959), 2, 266.

10. R. Peter Gillis and Thomas R. Roach, "American Influence on Conservation in Canada," *Journal of Forest History* 30 (Oct. 1986) 160–161, 162, 163, 171–173

11. Gillis and Roach, "Beginnings of a Movement," 132; MacEachern, "Conservation Movement."

12. Brown, "Doctrine of Usefulness," 48–49.

13. C. J. Taylor, "Legislating Nature: The National Parks Act of 1930," in Rowland Lorimer et al., eds., *To See Ourselves/To Save Ourselves: Ecology and Culture in Canada* (Montreal 1991), 126.

14. *Rocky Mountains Park Act*, S.C. 1887, c. 32, s. 4.

15. Brown, "Doctrine of Usefulness," 49.

16. Brown, "Doctrine of Usefulness," 48.

17. Marty, *A Grand and Fabulous Notion*, 98.

18. MacEachern, "Conservation Movement."

19. Marty, *A Grand and Fabulous Notion*, 64.

20. Foster, *Working for Wildlife*, 31.

21. Clifford Sifton, *Review of Work of the Commission of Conservation* (Montreal 1917), 5–14.

22. Tina Loo, *States of Nature: Conserving Canada's Wildlife in the Twentieth Century* (Vancouver 2006), 4.

23. This act prohibited the killing some animals, like the wood bison, and imposed restricted hunting seasons for other less threatened species. Barry Potyondi, *Wood Buffalo National Park: An Historical Overview and Source Study* (Parks Canada 1979), vii, 64.

24. In the Department of Agriculture report *Canada: Its History, Productions and Natural Resources*, the chapter entitled "Animal Life and Hunting Grounds" in both the 1886 and 1904 editions are exactly the same, showing that in nearly twenty years, little thought had been given to investigating the importance of wild animals. *Canada: Its History, Productions and Natural Resources* (Canada 1886; rev. ed. 1904, 1906).

25. John F. Reiger, *American Sportsmen and the Origins of Conservation* (New York 1975), 26, 52; James B. Trefethen, *An American Crusade For Wildlife* (New York 1975), 81, 84.

26. Thomas R. Dunlap, *Saving America's Wildlife* (Princeton 1988), 6, 7.

27. Tina Loo, "Making a Modern Wilderness: Conserving Wildlife in Twentieth-Century Canada," *Canadian Historical Review* 82 (March 2001), 96–97. Quebec was unique in that private fish-and-game clubs, and not the provincial government, began to carry out measures to manage wildlife. Beginning in 1883, Quebec allowed clubs to lease crown land at a low price. In exchange, these clubs were to take responsibility of managing the wildlife and fish stocks on their leaseholds. Loo, "Making a Modern Wilderness," 97.

28. George Altmeyer, "Three Ideas of Nature in Canada, 1893–1914," in Gaffield and Gaffield, eds., *Consuming Canada*, 107–108.

29. W. F. Lothian, *A History of Canada's National Parks*, vol. 4 (Ottawa 1981), 16.

30. Lothian, *A History of Canada's National Parks*, 17.

31. Karen Wonders, "A Sportsman's Eden: A Wilderness Besieged," pt. 2, *Beaver* 79 (Dec. 1999–Jan. 2000), 31–32.

32. Robert J. Burns, *Guardians of the Wild: A History of the Warden Service of Canada's National Parks* (Calgary 2000), 3–4.

33. Marty, *A Grand and Fabulous Notion*, 83.

34. Foster, *Working for Wildlife*, 57.

35. Foster, *Working for Wildlife*, 62.

36. Foster, *Working for Wildlife*, 62.

37. Graham MacDonald, *Science and History at Elk Island: Conservation Work in a Canadian National Park: 1914–1994* (Calgary 1994), 9–10.

38. F. A. Wyatt and J. D. Newton et al., *Soil Survey of Wainwright and Vermilion Sheets* (Edmonton 1944), 9. From 1914 until at least 1920, the Dominion government granted the Town of Wainwright the right to make test borings for natural gas within Buffalo National Park. It does not appear, however, that any strikes were made. Extract from LAC, Gas Report, J. B. Harkin to J. G. Mitchell, 11 Mar. 1914 and Commissioner to W. J. Blair, 14 Jun. 1919, Commissioner to Messrs. Shouldice and Farthing, 2 Sept. 1926, Parks Canada Files, BNP, RG 84, Vol. 983, File BU29, pt. 1.

39. Marsha Scribner, *Transitions: Commemorating Camp Wainwright's 50th Anniversary* (n.p.: Jostens, 1990), 28.

40. MacDonald, *Science and History at Elk Island*, 15.

41. Michael Clayton Wilson, "Bison in Alberta: Palaeontology, Evolution, and Relationships with Humans," in John Foster, Dick Harrison, and I. S. MacLaren, eds., *Buffalo* (Edmonton 1992), 5–6.

42. John E. Foster, "Introduction," in Foster, Harrison, MacLaren, eds., *Buffalo*, viii.

43. Andrew Isenberg, "The Returns of the Bison: Nostalgia, Profit, and Preservation," *Environmental History* 2 (April 1997), 181, 182.

44. I. S. MacLaren, "Buffalo in Word and Image: From European Origins to the Art of Clarence Tillenius," in Foster, Harrison, MacLaren, eds., *Buffalo*.

45. Hewitt, *Conservation of the Wild Life of Canada*, 113.

46. Marty, *A Grand and Fabulous Notion*, 80.

47. Foster, *Working for Wildlife*, 57–59.

48. Foster, *Working for Wildlife*, 66–73.

49. Lott, *American Bison*, 188; "Flathead Reservation Timeline," *Flathead Reservation Historical Society*, Montana Heritage Project, 2004 <http://www.flatheadreservation.org/timeline/timeline.html> (14 June 2004).

50. LAC, J. Obed Smith to W. D. Scott, 20 Nov. 1905, Parks Canada Files, BNP, RG 84, Vol. 51, File BU209, pt. 1.

51. LAC, Perley Keyes to W. W. Cory and 1 Dec. 1905, W.W. Cory to Perley Keyes, 8 Jan. 1906, Parks Canada Files, BNP, RG 84, Vol. 51, File BU209, pt. 1.

52. Coder, "National Movement," 187.

53. Marty, *Grand and Fabulous Notion*, 85.

54. LAC, Benjamin Davis to Superintendent of Immigration, 6 Mar. 1906, W. W. Cory to W. D. Scott, 24 Mar. 1906 and Howard Douglas to W. W. Cory, 15 Jun. 1906, Parks Canada Files, BNP, RG 84, Vol. 51, File BU209, pt. 1.

55. LAC, D. W. Johnson for Commissioner to Michel Pablo, 17 Jul. 1913, Parks Canada Files, BNP, RG 84, Vol. 51, File BU209, pt. 3.

56. LAC, Howard Douglas to W. W. Cory, 1 Mar. 1907 and Howard Douglas to W. W. Cory, 27 Jul. 1907, Parks Canada Files, BNP, RG 84, Vol. 51, File BU209, pt. 1.

57. LAC, Howard Douglas to W. W. Cory, 27 Jul. 1907, Parks Canada Files, BNP, RG 84, Vol. 51, File BU209, pt. 1.

58. George Colpitts, *Game in the Garden: A Human History of Wildlife in Western Canada to 1940* (Vancouver 2002), 103–104.

59. LAC, Howard Douglas to W. W. Cory, 15 Jun. 1906, Parks Canada Files, BNP, RG 84, Vol. 51, File BU209, pt. 1.

60. LAC, Howard Douglas to W. W. Cory, 15 Jun. 1906, Parks Canada Files, BNP, RG 84, Vol. 51, File BU209, pt. 1.

61. LAC, "Protect the Buffalo," Newspaper Clipping, n.d., Parks Canada Files, BNP, RG 84, Vol. 51, File BU209, pt. 1.

62. LAC, Benjamin Davis to W. W. Cory, 2 Apr. 1907 and "Canada Buys Buffalo Herd," Parks Canada Files, BNP, RG 84, Vol. 51, File BU209, pt. 1.

63. LAC, Howard Douglas to W. W. Cory, 1 Mar. 1907, W. W. Cory to Howard Douglas 7 Mar. 1907, and Howard Douglas to W. W. Cory, 15 Jun. 1906, Parks Canada Files, BNP, RG 84, Vol. 51, File BU209, pt. 1. Even if the Canadian government had not agreed to purchase the entire herd, it likely would have had nothing to fear. Pablo distrusted the United States government, especially after a representative approached him with an offer of $25 per head for his bison, and only begrudgingly increased his offer to $75 per head. Coder, "National Movement," 178–79. The *Edmonton Bulletin* reported that when Pablo was informed shortly after this meeting that the Flathead reserve would be thrown open for settlement, he made a reasonable connection between this decision and the government representative who had pressed him to sell his bison at a low price; this act "greatly exasperated Pablo and clinched his decision not to sell his buffalo to Uncle Sam at any price." *Edmonton Bulletin*, 8 Nov. 1907, 11, D. J. Benham, "The Round Up of the Second Herd of Pablo's Buffalo," quoted in Coder, "National Movement," 187.

64. LAC, Commissioner to John Halstead, 7 Aug. 1908, Parks Canada Files, BNP, RG 84, Vol. 52, File BU209, pt. 5.

65. LAC, Howard Douglas to Secretary of the Department of the Interior, 12 Aug. 1908 and F. H. Byshe to Deputy Minister, 19 Aug. 1908, Parks Canada Files, BNP, RG 84, Vol. 51, File BU209, pt. 2.

66. LAC, Rodolphe Boudreau to Minister of the Interior, Extract from the Report of the Committee of the Privy Council, approved by the Governor General on 31 Aug. 1907, Parks Canada Files, BNP, RG 84, Vol. 51, File BU209, pt. 1.

67. LAC, D. W. Johnson for the Commissioner to Michel Pablo, 17 Jul. 1913, Parks Canada Files, BNP, RG 84, Vol. 51, File BU209, pt. 3.

68. LAC, Howard Douglas to the Secretary, Department of the Interior, 23 Nov. 1910, Parks Canada Files, BNP, RG 84, Vol. 51, File BU209, pt. 3. The American Bison Society reported that Charles Conrad and his brother established their herd of buffalo with the purchase of 36 head in 1901 from Charles Allard's widow. George Bird Grinnell and Charles Sheldon, eds., *Hunting and Conservation: The Book of the Boone and Crockett Club* (New Haven 1925), 405–06. Therefore, the bison purchased by the Canadian government from Mrs. Conrad were originally Pablo-Allard bison.

69. Foster, *Working for Wildlife*, 66.

70. LAC, Howard Douglas to W. W. Cory, 22 May 1907, Parks Canada Files, BNP, RG 84, Vol. 51, File BU209, pt. 1.

71. LAC, Howard Douglas to W. W. Cory, 11 Jun. 1907, Parks Canada Files, BNP, RG 84, Vol. 51, File BU209, pt. 1, and RG 84, Vol. 981, BU2[548608], pt. 1.

72. LAC, Clerk of the Privy Council to the Minister of the Interior, 27 Mar. 1913, RG 84, Vol. 982, File BU2[548608], pt. 2.

73. MacDonald, *Science and History at Elk Island*, 31.

74. LAC, Howard Douglas to W. W. Cory, 15 Jun. 1906, Parks Canada Files, BNP, RG 84, Vol. 51, File BU209, pt. 1.

75. For example, *Montreal Weekly Witness*, 13 Jun. 1916, "World's Greatest Buffalo Herd is Now in Canada, at Wainwright Park, Alberta," and *Toronto Telegram*, 30 Jun. 1916, "Canada's Big Buffalo Herd," in LAC, Parks Canada Files, BNP, RG 84, Vol. 53, File BU232, pt. 1.

76. Hewitt, *Conservation of the Wild Life of Canada*, 135.

77. C. Gordon Hewitt, "The Coming Back of the Bison," *Natural History* 19 (Dec. 1919), 560.

78. LAC, J. B. Harkin to W. W. Cory, 4 Feb. 1916, Parks Canada Files, BNP, RG 84, Vol. 53, File BU232, pt. 1.

79. LAC, Memorandum to Maxwell Graham, 17 Jan. 1916, Parks Canada Files, BNP, RG 84, Vol. 53, File BU232, pt. 1.

80. LAC, Memorandum to Maxwell Graham, 17 Jan. 1916, Parks Canada Files, BNP, RG 84, Vol. 53, File BU232, pt. 1.

81. LAC, Commissioner to W. J. Blair, 23 Jun. 1920, Parks Canada Files, BNP, RG 84, Vol. 53, File BU232, pt. 2.

82. LAC, Memorandum to J. G. Mitchell, 7 Mar. 1914 and John E. Sloat to Dr. Roche, 25 Feb. 1914, Parks Canada Files, BNP, RG 84, Vol. 155, File U209, pt. 1. The Scotty Phillips buffalo bison were progeny of the Frederick Dupree herd. Coder, "National Movement," 26.

83. LAC, Note from J. B. Harkin on Letter, Commissioner to J. G. Mitchell, 19 Feb. 1920, Parks Canada Files, BNP, RG 84, Vol. 155, File U209, pt. 1.

CHAPTER THREE

A Well-Run Ranch[1]

*Domestication and Commercialization of the Plains
Bison in Buffalo National Park, 1920–1939*

WITH THE PURCHASE OF THE PABLO PLAINS BISON HERD from the Flat-head Valley of Montana in 1907, the Dominion government embarked on the largest wildlife saving effort of the early 20th century. From the beginning, however, both the structure of Buffalo National Park and the management of the plains bison herd resembled a domestic cattle operation. Ellis Treffry, son of Vern Treffry (who was employed as park rider during fall roundups from 1921 to 1939), described the park as "essentially a big ranch, other than they had buffalo instead of cattle."[2]

The ranch-style management of the bison at Wainwright is not surprising. Those in the administration of the Department of the Interior and, after 1911, the Parks Branch, depended on agricultural knowledge to guide the bison effort at Buffalo National Park. In fact, in many of the early saving efforts, wild animals were domesticated in order to save them and increase their numbers. The bison herd increased rapidly in the first decade of the effort (1909–19). The Parks Branch, however, was initially hesitant to implement policies to curtail the growing size of the herd. In hindsight, their approach to the overpopulation problem was perhaps too cautious. Conflicting ideas of how to manage the rapid growth of the bison herd ethically and then further delays due to deliberations about how to make the herd most profitable created an even greater crisis.

By the 1920s, the Parks Branch needed to make the growing herd financially useful in order to sustain the effort and the focus of the bison became a commercial venture. In the end, however, commercializing the herd came at a cost. While making the bison profitable was necessary to sustain the effort financially, the type of management that followed at Wainwright compromised the integrity of the species. Somewhere in the desperation to make the overgrown effort pay for itself, the bison herd, while technically already domesticated,[3] completely lost its wildness.

At the turn of the 20th century, saving wild animals, especially those species considered to be on the verge of extinction, was enacted in the spirit of utility. At this time, domesticating these animals was a way to ensure their permanence and would have been understood as a means of "preservation" as illustrated by C. "Buffalo" Jones's attempt to save wood bison and muskox. Jones, famous for the role he played in saving the plains bison from extinction in the 1880s, was worried about the welfare of the large mammals in northern Canada. He approached the Dominion government in 1899 with a proposal to capture some of these animals to save them from extinction. In a letter to the governor general he wrote, "It is of the greatest importance that Some of booth [sic] the buffalo or Bison and Musk Ox, and also a few Reindeer Should be domesticated and preserved, as no law can protect them against distructive Storms, Wolves, or hungry Indians, particularly the buffalo that are so near extinct in a wild state."[4] Although the expedition never came to fruition, it might be argued that the government approved the scheme because Jones agreed to donate half of the animals he captured to Rocky Mountains Park.[5] As William Pearce from the Department of the Interior wrote, "It would be a good thing to list the domestication of…these classes named, the Muskox in particular."[6]

The Dominion government continued to explore domestication schemes in the early 20th century. A 1922 Department of the Interior report investigated the potential of domesticating muskox and reindeer. These animals were not in danger of extinction, but the government hoped to safeguard them for future use since they were deemed a valuable meat supply. The hides of the animals and the wool of the muskox were also felt to have potential.[7]

Saving wild animals by the means of domestication was a product of the perception in the 19th century that once-abundant game populations could not survive the onslaught of development and settlement. The alarm was raised by the near extinction of the plains bison. If herds as vast and as important as the bison could disappear over mere decades, then all species were at risk of extinction. Of the near annihilation of the southern bison herd, zoologist William Hornaday wrote, "With such a lesson before our eyes, confirmed in every detail by living testimony, who will dare to say that there will be an elk, moose, caribou, mountain sheep, mountain goat, antelope, or black-tail deer left alive in the United States in a wild state fifty years from this date, ay, or even twenty-five?"[8] Given the changes to the North American West, the only way that the plains bison could be saved was by raising them in private herds to increase their numbers and protect them from poachers. Thus, the five individual efforts that are credited with saving a remnant of these animals from the decimation of the late 19th century were actually domestication efforts where humans intervened and raised bison in captivity to ensure the future survival of the species.

All five of the individual efforts credited with saving the plains bison from extinction (James McKay and Charles Alloway of Manitoba, Frederick Dupree of South Dakota, Charles Goodnight of Texas, Charles "Buffalo" Jones of Kansas, and Samuel Walking Coyote of Montana) captured bison calves when it looked as if the species might disappear without some intervention. In each case, the captured calves were fed domestic cow milk to sustain them on the journey back to the respective ranches. Once there, the calves were adopted by domestic cows and reared in captivity. In the case of the McKay-Alloway, Dupree, and Goodnight herds, crossbreeding between the bison and domestic herds resulted when the two species ranged in enclosures together. It is unclear whether Jones, who captured the most calves (56), grazed his bison with cattle, but it is probable that he did. He was very interested in crossbreeding, as is evidenced by his 1889 purchase of Colonel Samuel Bedson's herd from Stony Mountain, Manitoba, which consisted of both purebred and hybrid bison.[9]

In comparison to these early private initiatives to save the plains bison, the Pablo-Allard herd, at first glance, appears to have been managed with much less attention to domestication. The herd was considered to be the last free-roaming plains bison herd on the continent—a key factor in the Dominion government's interest in the animals. When examining the herd in June 1906, Howard Douglas, superintendent of Rocky Mountains Park, was impressed with how the herd had flourished under natural conditions. The range on which the bison grazed was not fenced. Rather, the herd was contained in the Round Butte area by natural barriers: "On the east were the majestic Mission Mountains, on the north was Flathead Lake, on the west were the Bitter Root Mountains, and to the south lay the Jocko Valley."[10] The herd also followed annual movements: it grazed in the valley in the summer and migrated across the Pend d'Orielle River to the mountains for the winter. The herd was never supplemented with hay and Douglas was pleased to find that Pablo "never [gave] any attention to the herd, and they [had] increased without any effort on his part."[11] This notion that the herd required low maintenance was substantiated by a 1902 article in *Forest and Stream*, which stated that although Pablo had "buffalo herders" to keep the herd within the range, they had little work to do but watch it.[12]

While the Pablo-Allard bison-saving effort initially appears to have been less intrusive when compared to the other early efforts, in reality its management can hardly be considered much different from that of domestic range cattle—unsurprising, since both Allard and Pablo were successful ranchers. That the Pablo herd had been managed like range cattle is clear as Douglas noticed, on inspecting the herd in 1906, that there were 50 bison steers among the 300 head.[13] In 1923, when an aged bison steer was slaughtered, an ear tag bearing the number "75" was discovered.[14] In 1932, two more ear tags, numbers "39" and "79," were found when two original Pablo bison were slaughtered.[15] As well, A. G. Smith, superintendent of Buffalo National Park, noted in 1923 that a number of the old bulls sported a slit in one of their ears, which suggested that at one time a number of the original Montana herd had been tagged in a similar fashion.[16]

Did Allard and Pablo purchase the herd with the intention of saving the species from extinction? Allard, described as an aggressive, farseeing, shrewd businessman, seems to have known the value of the animals. While it is not clear which of the two ranchers negotiated with Samuel Walking Coyote for his bison, knowledge of Allard's personality has led people to believe he initiated the sale.[17] The suggestion that Allard's motives for securing the herd were based on knowledge of the bison's value as a financial investment is substantiated by the fact that he continued to purchase additional bison, including the 1893 purchase of 26 purebred bison and 18 hybrids from C. "Buffalo" Jones.[18] Allard also took pleasure in displaying his bison; he took some to Butte, Montana, to an exhibition on "wild west riding sports" and had planned to take some to World's Fair in Chicago.[19]

While Pablo is described as a successful rancher, he also exhibited altruistic motives behind acquiring the bison. Tony Barnaby, Pablo's son-in-law, suggested that Pablo felt indebted to the species.[20] His love for the animals was evident when he realized that he would be forced to sell his portion of the herd. When he was unable to persuade the United States government to buy the herd and protect them, Pablo was "moved to manly tears,"[21] according to Barnaby. While bison had been sold from the herd in many small and some large sales, these sales seem to have been negotiated by Allard. There is no evidence that Pablo sold any of his bison before he was forced to by the government's decision that his grazing land was to be opened for settlement.[22] Pablo also put extra effort and expense into shipping his herd to Alberta. He built additional corrals out on the range and constructed cages that were drawn by 30, four-horse teams to transport the bison that were unwilling to

The park riders participated in the annual round-ups. Beginning in 1922, with the exception of four years, the bison were culled annually to reduce the size of the herd. This photo was taken circa 1928. From left to right: Blake Sharp, Frank Love, Bob Hyatt, Ray Sharp, Warren Blinn, George Armstrong, Vern Treffry, Bert Kitchen, and Bud Cotton. Photo by William Carsell.

be driven to Ravalli, where the rail cars were located.[23] Douglas noted some of the huge personal expense that Pablo accepted:

> I am perfectly satisfied, as I always have been, that the Old Man will ship every hoof he agreed to, and only those who know from personal experience what a huge undertaking it is, will ever credit him with the plucky fight he has put up, and the enormous expense incurred, which I should say would be about half what he is getting for the herd."[24]

From the beginning, the bison herd at Buffalo National Park was managed more like range cattle, like all previous bison-saving efforts. The experience and background of the park's administration played a role in this. All those administering the effort and those consulted for advice on the management of the herd were familiar with and/or had knowledge of agricultural management methods. Rocky Mountains Park Superintendent Howard Douglas was the man who spearheaded the purchase of the bison and the establishment of Buffalo National Park. His keen business sense, apparent at the time of the bison's purchase, can be traced to his experience of owning a general store and a coal and wood company; however, he also had a background in agriculture. He was raised on a family farm in Halton, Ontario, where he worked until he was 21.[25] J. B. Harkin, who was appointed commissioner of the newly formed Parks Branch in 1911, was the most influential person in the administration of the national parks system; his most significant role was overseeing the policy that affected the herd's management. Harkin's background was primarily in politics. He was a newspaperman, a parliamentary correspondent, and later a private secretary to Ministers of the Interior Clifford Sifton and Frank Oliver. While it appears that Harkin had little agricultural experience, Alan MacEachern argues that Harkin should not be solely credited with conceptualizing national park policies. While these are attributed to Harkin, policies were often drafted by his assistants and thus were a reflection of the beliefs of the Parks Branch as a whole.[26] Hoyes Lloyd, administrator of the Migratory Bird Regulations at the Parks Branch, was one assistant whom MacEachern names as drafting policy for Harkin. Trained as a chemist, Lloyd had worked closely with veterinarians and milk inspectors to eradicate the problem of bovine tuberculosis, a condition that posed a danger to Ontario's milk supply.[27] It is also clear from correspondence found in the Buffalo National Park files that Harkin often

The park farm, located in the southeastern part of Buffalo National Park, was the centre of the agricultural operations for the park. The hay meadows nearby provided a source of winter feed for buffalo as well as horses and livestock used at the park. An additional six-hundred acres were cultivated and provided oats for Buffalo National Park and other national parks. Photo by J. H. Gano.

consulted Maxwell Graham, Chief of Park Animals, for his opinion. Graham was trained at Ontario's Agricultural College in Guelph and farmed for six years before moving to Ottawa.[28]

Those working most closely with the bison at the local park level were also familiar with agricultural life. While little is known about Superintendent A. G. Smith's credentials, the wardens and park riders all had ranching experience. Bud Cotton, long-time warden at the park, moved from Sherbrooke, Quebec when he was sixteen and worked as a cowpuncher on some ranching operations in southern Alberta before he started at Buffalo National Park in 1913.[29] Of his park riders, Cotton stated: "All...had handled cattle and knew ranch routine, from branding to round-up."[30] Since the work of a park rider was seasonal, many had their own operations, which they tended to when not working at the park.

As little was known about wildlife science until the 1930s,[31] the Parks Branch turned to sources knowledgeable in domestic animal management and relied heavily on the Department of Agriculture for advice on managing the bison. Parks Branch officials frequently consulted with the Department of Agriculture for their opinions on different policies and the health of animals,[32] especially after the cattalo experiment began in 1916. Furthermore, local park officials often sought advice from the veterinarian in Wainwright regarding maintenance of the herd, whether it be to diagnose sick animals or to perform post-mortems.[33]

The structure and organization of Buffalo National Park also took on other characteristics of a domestication project. The preparations for the new park at Wainwright seem almost to have been modeled on a large ranch operation. Despite the fact that the area set aside south of Wainwright was a vast amount of territory, comprising 100,000 acres, settlement surrounded the park area and the park needed to be fenced. Before the park opened, Howard Douglas also requested cost estimates for a "house for [a] caretaker, corralls, stables, horses, saddles, and feed for Winter of 1908 & 1909."[34] The park farm, located in the southeastern portion of the park, oversaw all the agricultural operations. It had a "[p]ermanent farm staff, including the park supervisor, one park warden, blacksmith's handyman, barn worker and six teamsters."[35] Employees were assigned to various duties, including repairing fences, plowing miles of fireguards, harvesting crops in the summer months, and hauling hay to the bison in the winter. The park was self-sufficient in that it grew its own crops to feed the bison:

Six hundred acres were farmed in grain, grass and legume rotation…
Usually 300 to 400 acres of oats were grown, rotated each year with
40 to 50 acres of sweet clover for fertility and hay and 100 to 150 acres
of grass for soil fiber and hay. The oats supplied grain and oat straw…
One of the main summer activities of the park farm staff was cutting
and stacking approximately 1,500 tons of hay during July to September. Hay was obtained from the floodable meadows along the Ribstone Creek. These meadows were either flooded naturally or could be
flooded manually each spring ensuring a good stand of high quality
hay each year.[36]

Even everyday operations referenced known agricultural methods. Maxwell Graham considered ranching techniques to be the best way to care for bison. He recommended that the local employees adhere to "methods pursued by intelligent ranch owners, and which [consist] mainly in close observation of the herd, the supplying of necessary rock salt, watching for fever ticks, and above all segregation of those animals who appear diseased."[37] From early on, the herd was continually subjected to human intervention. Working with bison was dangerous. The animals were quite unruly and it was in the best interests of those working with the bison that the herd be domesticated. In 1913, Bernard Hervey, Chief Superintendent of National Parks, recommended a proposal to pacify the herd. Park riders were to ride among the herd on a daily basis and cut a few animals out of the herd so that the bison would become familiar with this routine: "Conditions are exactly the same with ranche [sic] cattle," he stated, "but by usage of seeing mounted men continually amongst them they soon learn that they are there for their protection and will not molest the riders who sought to save one of their number in distress."[38] Whether Hervey's recommendation was followed and, if so, how long it continued is unknown. Yet it is clear that the bison continued to be handled as cattle since the herd was driven at least annually, from the summer range, an enclosure that comprised most of the park, to the winter quarters, a smaller range in the southern portion of the park, where they were fed hay during the winter months.[39] Furthermore, the annual population count would have required handling of the herd.[40]

The management governing Buffalo National Park would also have adhered to known ranching methods. While it is unclear when the sex ratio (two cows to one bull) was applied at Buffalo National Park, an awareness of the importance of a sex ratio can be seen at the purchase.[41] The sex and age of animals shipped from Montana were recorded, and it appears that it was believed that the ratio of cows to bulls had a direct influence on the rate of the herd's propagation. The adult stock from the first shipment to Elk Island, for example, consisted of 101 bulls, 18 steers, and 47 cows.[42] Of the second shipment, Douglas was pleased that the majority of the animals were female (169 of 211 head). "[I]t will place the herd now in Elk Island Park on a much better basis than it was after the first shipment...I might add," he continued, "that the cows are all prime young stock and the increase in the next few years should be very satisfactory."[43] The same idea is echoed again in 1912. Maxwell Graham seemed to attribute the lack of increase in the bison herd to an improper ratio. He stated, "from our records here it would appear that approximately over 1/2 of the entire buffalo herd, now in our Parks, consists of males, and further that more than 1/6 of these males are absolutely aged[;] this will probably explain why the natural increase has not been more than it has in the past."[44]

This policy of maintaining a proper sex ratio led to even greater control of the breeding stock. By 1914, park officials began to express concern over the sex ratio since it was believed that the herd possessed too many bulls.[45] When they introduced a policy to dispose of some excess bulls, the Parks Branch became involved, in a sense, in selecting which animals and characteristics would be used for breeding purposes. While this practice raises the broader issue of gene selection, which is too complex to address here, it is important to note that such decisions contributed to domestication. While injured or older bulls, no longer considered useful, were disposed of,[46] the selection of particular bulls also determined the docility of the herd. "Bolivar," an older bison, was disposed of in 1918 more for his bad temper than his physically unfit condition. He was described as being "of the genuine wild beast variety...and absolutely refuse[d] to be frightened, controlled or subdued."[47] Indeed, the department seemed interested in breeding more docile bison.

As the park had no stream of revenue, for no admission fee was charged at the park, it was in the Parks Branch's best interest to dispose of these excess old and injured bulls in a profitable manner.[48] They decided to wait until winter when the robes would be prime and when the meat "might profitably be sold to the public around Christmas time."[49] Certainly, disposing of the bison and profiting from them at the same time would have been seen as an acceptable practice, in line with concept of conservation and planned and controlled resource use directing the park system at that time.[50]

By 1919, officials believed that Buffalo National Park had an excess of 1,000 bulls.[51] Instead of culling this excess, the department first looked to museums and zoological collections in the United States and Canada as suitable outlets for the disposal of the bison. While there seemed to be some interest in securing specimens for mounting purposes, there was no interest in securing any live bulls.[52] One of the main reasons for this lack of interest, made clear by William Hornaday, director of the New York Zoological Society, was that the asking price of $250 was too high. He informed them that the market was already saturated with bison in the eastern United States, and that the prices for both bulls and cows had dropped by 50 per cent.[53] Given that there was little market for live bison, other avenues, such as establishing other bison parks on the Prairies, were suggested.[54] However, these schemes were often accompanied by an even greater financial obligation that the department was not in the position to entertain.

The herd continued to increase, and the Parks Branch explored other options to reduce the growing herd. The proposition of allowing sportsmen to shoot bison, and thereby bring in substantial revenue, was never entertained because J. B. Harkin believed that it would invite too much criticism.[55] However, selling excess bison bulls to interested farmers and ranchers was seriously considered. Harkin believed buyers would be more than willing to purchase a bull for $250, making this one of the easiest ways by which to recoup some revenue.[56] While the scheme never came to fruition, Gordon Hewitt, Dominion entomologist, also endorsed the scheme and argued that farmers should be allowed to benefit from the value of the bison:

> The greatest value of the buffalo, however, lies in the possibility of its domestication. This may appear to be a novel idea, but I am convinced that its acceptance and adoption would result in inestimable benefit to the Prairie Provinces and the country as a whole. The greatest need in the Prairie Provinces is an increase in its beef-producing capacity. The buffalo is an animal which offers great possibilities, being pre-eminently suited to prairie conditions, and at the same time it produces a robe of no small commercial value.[57]

Naturally, the Department of Agriculture was very much in favour of making the bison beneficial for a different reason. Dr. Tolmie, minister of Agriculture, was very interested in the hybrid experiments and suggested selling surplus bison to farmers and ranchers. While he thought that the potential obstacles that would be encountered in crossbreeding should be made clear to purchasers, he also believed that private trials would give "many ranchers in the section an opportunity of experimenting under practical ranch conditions."[58]

Maxwell Graham, Chief of Park Animals, was very enthusiastic about the idea of a crossbreeding experiment. He proposed a cyclical breeding system that would not only recoup the costs of disposing of surplus bison, but also, in the long term, place the bison herd on a revenue basis. Once the correct ratio of the herd had been maintained in the park, all breeding females could be "placed with half their number of selected bulls" in one area. The rest of the "young stock" not yet ready for breeding could be placed in a second area, and steers and cows not selected for breeding in a third area for the purpose of beefing them. He believed that "[b]y following the above practice the increase of the herd will yield a steady revenue, while the total increase of breeding stock will be very gradual." Furthermore, he believed, the "perpetuation of the bison would be assured to a much greater degree" if the main herd was split and animals were distributed to farmers, ranchers, and other parks.[59]

It is surprising that the government never pursued the idea of selling bison to ranchers and farmers, especially since, in the mid-1920s, the United States had a policy of donating bison, at the cost of capturing and crating, to people who made applications.[60] While Harkin initially seemed to be exploring the idea, in the end this method of reducing the surplus bison was rejected for several reasons. First, the Department of Agriculture was already carrying out these experiments. Since these trials were in the early stages, and required expert advice, he felt amateur experiments by farmers, ranchers would be doomed to failure, and any negative publicity would adversely affect the government hybrid experiment at Wainwright.[61] Second, if the branch distributed bison to private individuals, they would not be able protect the park herds from poachers because it would be difficult to prove whether a robe or head came from a private herd or one of the parks.[62] This rationalization points to the third and greater objection for not distributing bison to interested individuals: it would deprive "the Department of the virtual monopoly it now enjoys in the possession of the herds of bison administered by this Branch in our National Parks."[63] Clearly, Harkin viewed the surrender of this monopoly as a forfeiture of future revenue because the Parks Branch could benefit more by disposing of the bison themselves.

By the 1920s, the rapid growth of the bison herd was beginning to endanger the effort itself. While carrying capacity had yet to be determined, the herd was dangerously close to outgrowing the park (by the 1930s, the capacity of the park range under normal conditions had been judged to be 5,000 head).[64] As the management of the bison became more costly, the park was in need of revenue. To distribute bison to local ranchers would render the animals commonplace and leave the Parks Branch without its only revenue source. With 1,000 bulls to dispose of in 1919, Maxwell Graham pointed out that if the highest prices could be achieved from sale of the meat, heads, and hides, the profit would be considerable.[65] In 1921, Harkin reported with enthusiasm the financial benefit that could be realized from the growing bison herd: "The numbers have been increasing so rapidly that we have been compelled to look toward—I might almost say—the commercialization of the herds…what we started off to do from a purely sentimental standpoint may prove to be a valuable commercial proposition. For instance, there is a market for the herds—apparently a better paying market than we had ever anticipated."[66]

The Parks Branch, however, took too long deliberating over the proper way to realize this potential revenue. One obstacle lay in the fact that Buffalo National Park had been initiated and promoted as a saving effort, so officials had to be careful to deal with the overpopulation problem in a way that would not alienate the public. More importantly, the Parks Branch wanted to ensure that the bison products, of which the most important was the meat, were marketed properly. It was clear when the department finally considered slaughtering bison for food purposes in 1918 that disposing of excess bison was going to be a long-term problem. Since only bulls were to be disposed of in the beginning, Harkin was concerned that the meat proposition not be given a "black-eye": "We have to look forward to the development of a buffalo meat trade as a high priced one and of course we cannot take any chances of damning it at the start by disposing of any meat to the public which would not be attractive."[67]

This cautious approach to reducing the herd only served to create greater problems. In hindsight, it probably would have been wiser if an overtly commercial policy, even if more controversial, had been followed from 1916, when it was first realized that the herd was too large. While the Parks Branch deliberated, the herd continued to increase. By 1922–23, the size of the herd, which numbered 6,780 bison (see Table 2), began to threaten the park's ecological viability.

TABLE 2: BISON POPULATION CENSUS, 1922–32	
Year	*Number of Bison*
1922–23	6,780
1923–24	6,655
1924–25	8,267
1925–26	8,832
1926–27	6,026
1927–28	4,241
1928–29	4,300
1929–30	5,016
1930–31	6,231
1931–32	6,331

Source: LAC, Memorandum to J. B. Harkin, 15 Feb. 1933, Parks Canada Files, Buffalo National Park, RG84, Vol. 50, BU217, pt. 1.

By 1922, commercializing the herd was the only option left to save the effort from financial ruin. In response to a letter from Colin Moncrieff, who believed the surplus bison should be released rather than slaughtered, Harkin wrote:

> There is another consideration and that is, that the government to date has spent a very considerable amount of money for the purpose of preserving the buffalo. Conditions have become such that the government can safely market a very considerable number of the animals each year and get a financial return to help pay the bills incurred for the purpose of preserving the animal from extinction. I am inclined to think that public opinion will endorse the idea that commercialization of the herd without interfering with the preservation of the species will be amply justified.[68]

Although it was necessary to dispose of about 1,000 bulls in 1922, no large-scale effort to reduce the herd took place until 1923. The slaughter in 1922 was actually a smaller experiment made in order to test the market for bison meat.[69] The delay can be attributed to the department's taking great pains to make the bison as profitable as possible. Harkin stated, "our only hope for any considerable profit in the disposal of meat will be to put it on as a luxury and not in competition with beef. In other words we must demand a price considerably higher than the current price of beef."[70] Harkin knew that creating a market for bison products was going to be difficult and costly.[71] A. S. Duclos of Edmonton Cold Meat Storage secured the tender for the slaughter that first year. He made it clear that since the slaughter would become an annual practice, it was important that this first experiment profit both the department and the buyer.[72]

Not only did the delay in implementing a large-scale reduction of the herd allow the bison population to continue to increase, but the first experimental slaughter of 265 animals proved that it was going to be more difficult to market the meat than the Parks Branch had anticipated. Since the park needed to get rid of mature bulls, the biggest question was whether or not the meat would be attractive for consumption. Much like the meat from older domestic bulls, however, bison bull meat was found to be tough and unpalatable. Even meat from younger bulls was unsatisfactory, as bison meat used for a barbeque in Jasper proved.[73] This problem with the meat's quality posed a huge problem, and the Parks Branch was forced to find other ways to dispose of it profitably. Since only 200 pounds of an average 700 pound dressed bull could be considered choice meat, Harkin thought that the poorer quality cuts could be made into pemmican to be used as a trading item in the north, rather than risk marketing all the meat.[74]

A second, unexpected drawback from this experimental slaughter was that a high percentage of the carcasses, 61 out of the 264, were condemned.[75] This result not only created a setback in the plan to market the meat as a luxury, but also cost the department extra money, as the possibility of condemned carcasses was overlooked in the contract; dressing carcasses that were essentially useless cost just as much and took the same amount of time as dressing good carcasses.[76] While it is not clear whether or not condemned meat was tested in the experimental year, in the 1923–24 slaughter the meat was condemned because of disease.[77] This issue would cause widespread problems for the park in the future. The presence of disease not only harmed the herd, but also hindered the sale of bison meat products.

In the 1920s, when it was first discovered that the meat of older bulls would generate no demand, the Parks Branch experimented with creating steers to improve meat quality. Relying on the cattle industry's practice of improving the palatability of meat by castrating domestic bulls, Graham gave his support for such experiments as early as 1919: "In the case of young bulls prime beef of high quality could be made of these if such bulls were turned into steers and later beefed at three or four years of age."[78] In 1923, eleven calves were castrated. While the results did not prove profitable enough to warrant the continuation of the experiment,[79] the willingness to go to such lengths to make the bison herd more profitable shows the change of emphasis, from a saving effort to a business venture, taking place at Buffalo National Park.

The Parks Branch also began to explore the practice of selective breeding to improve the breeding stock of the herd and the quality of beef and hides. While the herd was never healthy enough in later years to implement a full-fledged policy, in 1932, A. G. Smith, reflecting on the management of the herd, stated:

> the thought of selective breeding is not a new one with us as for a number of years we have carried on with this idea in mind…
>
> It has been our policy each slaughter when the animals are being put through the corrals for the purpose of selecting beef stock to discard the weaklings and undesirable breeders from the herd, both male and female, and hold for breeding stock animals of good type and appearance.[80]

As the herd increased, the problem moved beyond disposing of excess bulls. It became necessary to reduce the population as a whole, both males and females. This action, however met with public protest; humane societies protested the killing of cows that were in calf. That the Parks Branch remained aloof from these protests illustrates how the effort shifted from a saving endeavour to a commercial venture focussed on gaining profit. In a letter to Harkin, James Smart of the Parks Branch stated, "To the practical stockmen, this is a joke and I see no reason why we should not treat the buffalo herd in the same way as a rancher treats his herd of domestic stock."[81]

Ultimately, commercializing the herd did not alleviate the park's financial problem, although in the short term, the effort appeared to bear some fruit. While sales of bison robes had not been very successful, Harkin was pleased with the meat returns from the first large-scale slaughter. He wrote, "I am beginning to think that the commercial returns from the slaughtering of the buffalo on the whole are going to be so satisfactory that as a pure matter of business it may be desirable to adhere to slaughtering as the best means for keeping the herd within reasonable numbers."[82] Even though the robes were not selling, they were not perishable and could be stored indefinitely.[83] However, the department decided not to slaughter any animals in the winter of 1924; it appears that the main reason for cancelling the slaughter was financial. Revenue from commercial sales was insufficient to sustain the effort, and another solution to the herd's growth had to be found.

Of interest, the suggestion to ship some of the excess herd north was first raised by Maxwell Graham in September 1919. He recommended that excess plains bison from Wainwright be transplanted to the habitat of the wood bison near Fort Smith so that the two herds would eventually mix.[84] Dominion Parks Inspector H. E. Sibbald raised the proposal again in January 1923 and suggested bison be shipped to the newly formed Wood Buffalo Park.[85] Initially, Harkin opposed the idea, stating that the area in question was not under the jurisdiction of the Parks Branch, but rather the North West Territories and Yukon Branch. Furthermore, he believed transporting the bison would be an expensive undertaking: "Apart from that, however, what particular object is to be served? It is likely that by annually slaughtering one thousand animals, or thereabouts, at Wainwright, the Department will be able to secure a substantial revenue. In the present condition of the country financially it seems to me this would be better policy than spending more money to transport these animals to the north."[86]

In 1925, 1,654 Wainwright bison bound for Wood Buffalo National Park were branded with a "Gamb Joint W" brand on right shank to help distinguish them from their wood bison counterparts. Here, local rancher Harry Mabey brandishes the iron. After the first year, branding was discontinued due to the cost and protests by the SPCA.
Photo by William Oliver.

The slaughter, however, was cancelled again in 1925. Harkin stated, the Parks Branch had "absolutely no funds with which to carry on killing operations this Fall."[87] The existence of products still on hand from the 1923 slaughter suggests that the market for bison products had not been as lucrative as anticipated.[88] Thus, this new outlet for the excess bison began to look more appealing as a cost-saving measure for the Parks Branch; while shipping bison was an expensive undertaking that offered no potential revenue, the North West Territories Branch was assuming all the shipping costs after the bison had been loaded on the trains at Wainwright. It was estimated that for the first shipment it would cost the Parks Branch $20,000, or $10 per head. This estimate was based on 2,000 bison and included the cost of building the necessary infrastructure to corral and load the bison on the trains.[89] As the infrastructure was a one-time cost, future shipments would cost the department only about $5,000 for around 2,000 animals, or $2.50 per head.[90]

When Harkin stated that the decision to move the bison north was made with the best interests of the people of Canada in mind, he was clearly implying that this route was the least costly to the government.[91] Anticipating that once the bison were shipped north they would increase at the same rate as they had in Wainwright, Harkin believed they would contribute significantly to northern development as a food and fur supply for Natives, explorers, and prospectors.[92] Shipping the bison north also removed the surplus population from public view and awareness. Certainly, this option of disposing of the surplus animals would have been considered more acceptable to the general public than disposing of the animals by slaughter.

Shipping the bison north led to another management practice that was rooted firmly in the ranching tradition: branding the bison. Symbolically, this practice was the greatest proof that the status of bison's wildness had been totally diminished and that the animals were now considered mere range stock. Branding was introduced as a measure to maintain the integrity of the plains bison; the practice was desired by the North West Territories Branch to permit the wardens in Wood Buffalo National Park to distinguish between the plains and wood bison. However, in hindsight the practice served little purpose, given that this means of identifying the species did nothing to prevent the two types of bison from interbreeding. After consulting with Dr. G. Hilton, Veterinary Director General, Dr. J. C. Hargrave, Chief Inspector for the Health of Animals Branch in Alberta and Maxwell Graham, Chief of Wild Life Division, the Parks Branch went

From 1925–1928, 6,673 bison were shipped north to Wood Buffalo National Park in an attempt to reduce the overpopulated bison herd at Wainwright.

ahead with the scheme; 1,654 bison were branded by local rancher Harry Mabey with a "W" on their right shank.[93] Bison were only branded in 1925, the first year they were sent north. The procedure was discontinued, however, because it was too costly; the bison had to be segregated, fed additional hay, and held in corrals longer than otherwise necessary.[94] However, Warden Ray Sharp stated the administration stopped the practice when the SPCA in Edmonton found out and members of the organization came to the park and complained.[95]

The herd, from the beginning of the effort, had been moved annually between its summer and winter ranges. However, from 1922 onward, with the exception of two years, the park riders rounded up the herd on an annual basis for either slaughter or shipment in much the same way as was done with domestic cattle. A newspaper description of the 1925 roundup, while saturated with descriptions of "Wild West" thrills, sounds very much like an annual spring roundup on a ranch, with a bit more action. Park riders drove the charged herd to the corrals, ran them through the chutes to the squeeze where they were branded, and then loaded them into the cattle cars.[96] While only a portion of the herd was targeted in the roundups, the process affected the majority of the herd. For the roundup in 1926 for the northern shipment, A. G. Smith stated that 7,101 animals were passed through the corrals in order to segregate 1,903 bison.[97]

By 1926, it was apparent that shipping bison north was not alleviating the park's overpopulation problem. Smith estimated that even with that year's shipment, the natural increase was going to leave the park with almost twice the number of bison recommended for the park.[98] While shipments north continued for two more years (see Table 3), it became necessary to resume slaughtering, and the Parks Branch was once again faced with the problem of making this slaughter commercially viable.

By the 1930s, the market for bison meat had fallen, as the exceedingly low price offered by Burns and Company for the contract to slaughter the herd in 1933 indicates. Burns stated that even beef prices were low and earlier that year had suggested that tenders be called early to all the bidders to make provisions to distribute the meat months before the kill. Bison meat was no longer a novelty, and it was more difficult to market.[99] Once again, other avenues for offloading surplus meat were also explored. J. B. Harkin even approached Gainers, inquiring about experimenting with canned meat.[100]

It was, however, the use of bison meat for relief purposes that proved to be the most effective outlet. In 1933, the meat was used by the Department

TABLE 3: INVENTORY OF BISON SLAUGHTERED BY CONTRACT AND SHIPPED TO WOOD BUFFALO NATIONAL PARK, 1922–40

Year	Number of Bison Slaughtered	Year	Number of Bison Shipped to Wood Buffalo National Park
1922–23	265	1922	-
1923–24	*1,881	1923	-
1924–25	-	1924	-
1925–26	-	1925	1,634
1926–27	**2,001	1926	2,011
1927–28	1,000	1927	1,940
1928–29	-	1928	1,088
1929–30	525	1929	-
1930–31	67	1930	-
1931–32	1,534	1931	-
1932–33	1,216	1932	-
1933–34	2,000	1933	-
1934–35	1,000	1934	-
1935–36	†	1935	-
1936–37	1,522	1936	-
1937–38	2,020	1937	-
1938–39	1,200	1938	-
1939–40	2,910	1939	-

Source: LAC, Commissioner to Geo. B. Grinnell, 12 Jul. 1942, Parks Canada Files, BNP, RG 84, Vol. 53, File BU232, pt 3; LAC, J. B. Harkin to William Rowan, 23 Mar. 1929 and F. H. H. Williamson to V. W. Jackson, 17 Jun. 1937, Parks Canada Files, BNP, RG 84, Vol. 54, File BU232, pt. 4; LAC, J. B. Harkin to Canada Packers Limited, 21 Nov. 1935, Parks Canada Files, BNP, RG 84, Vol. 58, File BU299, pt. 11; LAC, "Approximate Census of Buffalo Herd, March 31 1938," Parks Canada Files, BNP, RG 84, Vol. 57, File BU299, pt. 13; LAC, Memorandum to Mr. Lloyd, 4 Jan. 1939, Parks Canada Files, BNP, RG 84, Vol. 58, File BU299, pt. 14; and LAC, Memorandum to Mr. Lloyd, 15 Jan. 1940, Parks Canada Files, BNP, RG 84, Vol. 58, File BU299, pt. 15.

* LAC, Commissioner to Geo. B. Grinnell, 12 Jul. 1924, Parks Canada Files, BNP, RG 84, Vol. 53, File BU232 pt 3. This letter states that the number of bison slaughtered in 1923–24 was 1,847.

** LAC, J. B. Harkin to William Rowan, 23 Mar. 1929, Parks Canada Files, BNP, RG 84, Vol. 54, File BU232, pt. 4. This letter states the number of bison slaughtered in 1926–27 was 2,013.

† There was no slaughter in 1935–36 because the abattoir at Buffalo National Park burned down.

of National Defence for national park relief camps, as well as for Inuit relief.[101] Meat was again distributed in this manner in the 1934–35 slaughter. When the Parks Branch wished to market the meat to the public again for the 1935–36 slaughter, Burns and Company warned that this would be difficult because the meat had been used for relief purposes. In any event, the slaughter did not take place as planned since the abattoir burned down that year.[102]

By the winter of 1938–39, the need to dispose of such high numbers of bison over the years had resulted in a herd composed mostly of younger animals. That year, most of the animals killed were yearlings and two-year olds. Burns and Company, who performed the slaughter that year, wrote:

> These young animals have not a good finish and do not show up to advantage when displayed on the retail counter. On the face of which it would seem that younger animals would be more desirable, particularly from the standpoint of tenderness, but the lack of finish which they showed this year has more than offset the desirability of them in eating qualities…In the past years Buffalo has been looked upon by a great many people as a desirable meat novelty, but certainly the quality of these younger animals, this year, did a great deal to dissipate this idea in the minds of the buying public, and we are of the opinion that serious damage could be done to the reputation of Buffalo if the slaughter of these younger animals continues.[103]

From the beginning, Buffalo National Park resembled a domestication effort, not unlike other early endeavours to save near-extinct species. While commercialization of the bison herd at Buffalo National Park was not a route that the Park Branch's had intended to follow, the rapid growth of the herd was not anticipated. Their cautious approach to curtailing this growth, however, resulted in an even greater overpopulation crisis. While the Parks Branch explored other avenues to downsize the herd, most of them were not viable and the first few culls were not effective. Shipping bison north, considered because it was the most economical solution, relieved the overpopulation problem only temporarily. The Parks Branch quickly found itself needing to introduce a cull to downsize the herd in a profitable manner, and the focus on saving the bison moved to the back burner. Unfortunately, the Parks Branch was never very successful at realizing any significant profit from its new bison venture.

The most significant tragedy at Buffalo National Park was the change in attitude towards the bison by those administering the effort at Buffalo

National Park. As the emphasis shifted from a saving effort to a commercial ranching business, the integrity of the bison as a species was compromised. In the 1920s, with the bison population exploding, the Parks Branch apparently believed that the saving of the species from extinction had been achieved and was no longer necessary. Again, in response to Colin Moncrieff's suggestion that the surplus bison be released, Harkin stated, "How to deal with the surplus animals now constitutes a real and pressing problem. The desirability of preserving the species from extinction is not a factor in this matter as I have already said the maintaining of the present herds [Buffalo and Elk Island] provides the guarantee against extinction."[104] Unfortunately, the shift in focus from a salvage effort to a business venture changed the value of the bison in the eyes of the Park Branch from a near-extinct, symbolic species to mere livestock, from which they could gain a profit.

Notes

1. Adeline Schleppe, personal interview, 11 Nov. 2002.

2. Ellis Treffry, personal interview, 11 Nov. 2002.

3. The *Oxford English Dictionary* defines "domesticate" as "to accustom (an animal) to live under the care and near the habitations of man; to tame or bring under control." *Oxford English Dictionary Online*, <http://dictionary. oed.com> (14 Jun. 2004). However, hybridization has also traditionally been defined as a domestication scheme. For the purpose of this study, a distinction will be made between "domestication," adapting and pacifying an animal to be controlled and used by humans, and "hybridization" or "crossbreeding," which will be addressed in chapter 5.

4. LAC, C. Jones to Governor General of Canada, 8 Nov. 1899, Parks Canada Files, BNP, RG 84, Vol. 155, File U209-1, pt. 1.

5. LAC, Memorandum to James A. Smart, 24 Nov. 1899, Parks Canada Files, BNP, RG 84, Vol. 155, File U209-1, pt. 1.

6. LAC, William Pearce to Lyndwode Pereira, 20 Nov. 1899, Parks Canada Files, BNP, RG 84, Vol. 155, File U209-1, pt. 1. The Dominion government agreed to allow Jones to capture ten bison, twenty-four musk oxen and twenty-six reindeer. LAC, Mr. Rothwell to C. J. Jones, 11 Jan. 1902, Parks Canada Files, BNP, RG 84, Vol. 155, File U209-1, pt. 1.

7. *Reindeer and Musk-Ox: Report of the Royal Commission upon the Possibilities of the Reindeer and Musk-Ox Industries in the Arctic and Sub-Arctic Regions* (Ottawa 1922), 7, 14, 15–16, 18, 21–22, 27–28.

8. Hornaday, *Extermination*, 391.

9. Coder, "National Movement," 1–45. Bedson's bison herd started with eight animals from the McKay-Alloway herd, which he purchased in 1880. Coder, "National Movement," 5.

10. Coder, "National Movement," 22.

11. LAC, Howard Douglas to the W. W. Cory, 15 Jun. 1906, Parks Canada Files, BNP, RG 84, Vol. 51, File BU209, pt. 1.

12. Whealdon et al., *I Will Be Meat for My Salish*, 86, 99.

13. LAC, Howard Douglas to the W. W. Cory, 15 Jun. 1906, Parks Canada Files, BNP, RG 84, Vol. 51, File BU209, pt. 1. The practice of castrating bulls to make steers is performed to make the animals more docile and improve the quality of meat.

14. LAC, Commissioner to Howard Douglas, 5 Mar. 1923, Parks Canada Files, BNP, RG 84, Vol. 51, File BU209, pt. 3.

15. LAC, R. Waddy to Veterinary Director General, 21 Jan. 1932, Parks Canada Files, BNP, RG 84, Vol. 58, BU299-2, pt. 1.

16. LAC, A.G. Smith to Commissioner, 21 Feb. 1923, Parks Canada Files, BNP, RG 84, Vol. 51, File BU209, pt. 3.

17. Whealdon et al., *I Will Be Meat for My Salish*, 86–87.

18. Coder, "National Movement," 39.

19. Whealdon et al., *I Will Be Meat for My Salish*, 86.

20. Whealdon et al., *I Will Be Meat for My Salish*, 83–84.

21. Whealdon et al., *I Will Be Meat for My Salish*, 84.

22. Whealdon et al., *I Will Be Meat for My Salish*, 84, 86, 87.

23. LAC, Michel Pablo to W. W. Cory, 18 Nov. 1908, Parks Canada Files, BNP, RG 84, Vol. 51, File BU209, pt. 2; Whealdon et al., *I Will Be Meat for My Salish*, 93.

24. LAC, Howard Douglas to W. W. Cory, 11 Nov. 1909, RG 84, Vol. 51, File BU209, pt. 2.

25. Foster, *Working for Wildlife*, 55.

26. MacEachern, *Natural Selections,* 29.

27. Foster, *Working for Wildlife*, 159.

28. Foster, *Working for Wildlife*, 97.

29. E. J. (Bud) Cotton, *Buffalo Bud: Adventures of a Cowboy* (Vancouver 1981), 6.

30. Bud Cotton, "Range Riding with Canada's Buffalo Herds," unpublished manuscript, personal collection of Adeline Schleppe, n.d.

31. MacDonald, *Science and History at Elk Island*, 31.

32. For example, Dr. S. E. Clarke, agrostologist, Dr. Frederick Torrance, veterinary director general, and Dr. Hargrave, inspector, all professionals from the Department of Agriculture, were consulted on matters pertaining to Buffalo National Park.

33. For example, Stan Wiley, the local veterinarian, was often called on to attend to the buffalo herd. Herb Dixon (grandson of Herb Walker, park farm superintendent), personal interview, 12 Feb. 2004.

34. LAC, Howard Douglas to the W. W. Cory, 22 Oct. 1907, Parks Canada Files, BNP, RG 84, Vol. 51, File BU209, pt. 1.

35. Treffry, personal interview, 11 Nov. 2002.

36. Treffry, personal interview, 11 Nov. 2002.

37. LAC, Maxwell Graham to Mr. Harkin, 3 Aug. 1912, Parks Canada Files, BNP, RG 84, Vol. 53, File BU232, pt. 1.

38. LAC, P. C. Bernard Hervey to J. B. Harkin, 10 May 1913, Parks Canada Files, BNP, RG 84, Vol. 53, File BU232, pt. 1. J. B. Harkin, on hearing of Hervey's recommendation, discouraged the procedure during calving period because he did not want to excite or harass the herd. LAC, Commissioner to P. C. Bernard Hervey, 20 May 1913, Parks Canada Files, BNP, RG 84, Vol. 53, File BU232, pt. 1.

39. LAC, J. B. Harkin to A. M. Comsia, 4 May 1935, Parks Canada Files, BNP, RG 84, Vol. 54, File BU232, pt. 4. Also see map entitled "Buffalo Park," 1926, in LAC, Parks Canada Files, BNP, RG 84, Vol. 50, File BU38, pt. 1.

40. For example, LAC, L. Pereira to Howard Douglas, 25 Mar. 1911, Parks Canada Files, BNP, RG 84, Vol. 53, File BU232, pt. 1.

41. In 1919, Harkin noted that experts in the United States had determined the proper sex ratio of bison to be one bull to two cows. LAC, J. B. Harkin to W. W. Cory, 3 Nov. 1919, Parks Canada Files, BNP, RG 84, Vol. 53, File BU232, pt. 2.

42. LAC, Howard Douglas to W. W. Cory, 11 Jun. 1907, Parks Canada Files, BNP, RG 84, Vol. 51, File BU209, pt. 1.

43. LAC, Howard Douglas to W. W. Cory, 22 Oct. 1907, Parks Canada Files, BNP, RG 84, Vol. 51, File BU209, pt. 1.

44. LAC, Maxwell Graham to Mr. Harkin, 3 Aug. 1912, Parks Canada Files, BNP, RG 84, Vol. 53, File BU232, pt. 1.

45. In this year, the composition of the herd was 500 bulls and 476 cows. Calves and yearlings numbered 470 and were of both sexes. LAC, Enclosure in Letter to Dr. Frederick Torrance, 10 Mar. 1914, Parks Canada Files, BNP, RG 84, Vol. 53, File BU232, pt. 1.

46. LAC, Letter to P. A. Taverner, 6 Dec. 1915, Parks Canada Files, BNP, RG 84, Vol. 53, File BU232, pt. 1.

47. LAC, *Rocky Mountain Courier*, 22 Feb. 1918, "Buffalo Herd is Thriving," Parks Canada Files, BNP, RG 84, Vol. 53, File BU232, pt. 1.

48. LAC, Mr. Courtice to J. B. Harkin, 13 Nov. 1916, Parks Canada Files, BNP, RG 84, Vol. 53, File BU232, pt. 1; LAC, F. H. H. Williamson to William Flemming, 29 Aug. 1940, Parks Canada Files, BNP, RG 84, Vol. 982, File BU2[548608], pt. 4.

49. LAC, Letter to P. A. Taverner, 6 Dec. 1915, Parks Canada Files, BNP, RG 84, Vol. 53, File BU232, pt. 1.

50. Taylor, "Legislating Nature," 127.

51. LAC, Commissioner to W. W. Cory, 3 Nov. 1919, Parks Canada Files, BNP, RG 84, Vol. 53, File BU232, pt. 2.

52. LAC, Maxwell Graham to J. B. Harkin, 1 Apr. 1919 and other correspondence, Parks Canada Files, BNP, RG 84, Vol. 53, File BU232, pt. 1.

53. LAC, William Hornaday to J. B. Harkin, 22 Sep. 1919, Parks Canada Files, BNP, RG 84, Vol. 53, File BU232, pt. 1.

54. Hewitt, *Conservation of the Wild Life of Canada*, 136.

55. LAC, J. B. Harkin to W. W. Cory, 21 Nov. 1922, Parks Canada Files, BNP, RG 84, Vol. 57, File BU299-1, pt. 1.

56. LAC, Commissioner to W. W. Cory, 3 Nov. 1919, Parks Canada Files, BNP, RG 84, Vol. 53, File BU232, pt. 2.

57. Hewitt, *Conservation of the Wild Life of Canada*, 136.

58. LAC, S. F. Tolmie to J. B. Harkin, 19 Nov. 1919, Parks Canada Files, BNP, RG 84, Vol. 53, File BU232, pt. 2.

59. LAC, Maxwell Graham to Commissioner, 17 Oct. 1919, Parks Canada Files, BNP, RG 84, Vol. 53, File BU232, pt. 1.

60. LAC, Hoyes Lloyd to Mr. Harkin, 8 Apr. 1926, Parks Canada Files, BNP, RG 84, Vol. 53, File BU232, pt. 3.

61. LAC, J. B. Harkin to R. A. Gibson, 13 Oct. 1920, Parks Canada Files, BNP, RG 84, Vol. 53, File BU232, pt. 2.

62. LAC, Commissioner to W. W. Cory, 22 Nov. 1919, Parks Canada Files, BNP, RG 84, Vol. 53, File BU232, pt. 2.

63. LAC, J. B. Harkin to R. A. Gibson, 13 Oct. 1920, Parks Canada Files, BNP, RG 84, Vol. 53, File BU232, pt. 2.

64. LAC, S. E. Clarke, "Report on Investigation of Pasture Conditions at Buffalo National Park," Sept. 1930, Parks Canada Files, BNP, RG 84, Vol. 50, File BU35, pt. 1.

65. LAC, Maxwell Graham to J. B. Harkin, 29 Sep. 1919, Parks Canada Files, BNP, RG 84, Vol. 53, File BU232, pt. 1.

66. LAC, [Irma] *Times*, 21 Oct. 1921, "Some Facts About Growth of Canada's Fine Buffalo Herd," Parks Canada Files, BNP, RG 84, Vol. 53, File BU232, pt. 3.

67. LAC, Commissioner to Superintendent, 29 Nov. 1918, Parks Canada Files, BNP, RG 84, Vol. 53, File BU232, pt. 1.

68. LAC, J. B. Harkin to Colin C. Moncrieff, 15 Dec. 1922, Parks Canada Files, BNP, RG 84, Vol. 52, File BU232-1, pt. 1.

69. LAC, J. B. Harkin to W. W. Cory, 21 Nov. 1922, Parks Canada Files, BNP, RG 84, Vol. 57, File BU299-1, pt. 1.

70. LAC, J. B. Harkin to W. W. Cory, 21 Nov. 1922, Parks Canada Files, BNP, RG 84, Vol. 57, File BU299-1, pt. 1.

71. LAC, J. B. Harkin to W. W. Cory, 6 Jun. 1922, Parks Canada Files, BNP, RG 84, Vol. 57, File BU299-1, pt. 1.

72. LAC, A. S. Duclos to Charles Stewart, 8 Jun. 1922, Parks Canada Files, BNP, RG 84, Vol. 57, File BU299-1, pt. 1.

73. LAC, Chief of the Animal Division to Commissioner, 17 Oct. 1919, Parks Canada Files, BNP, RG 84, Vol. 53, File BU232, pt. 1.

74. LAC, J. B. Harkin to W. W. Cory, 21 Nov. 1922, Parks Canada Files, BNP, RG 84, Vol. 57, File BU299-1, pt. 1.

75. LAC, Statement of Slaughtering Operations and Shipments, Buffalo Park, 1922–23, Parks Canada Files, BNP, RG 84, Vol. 57, File BU299-1, pt. 1.

76. LAC, J. B. Harkin to A. G. Smith, 24 Mar. 1923, Parks Canada Files, BNP, RG 84, Vol. 57, File BU299-1, pt. 1.

77. LAC, Memorandum to P. Marchand, 21 Jan. 1924, Parks Canada Files, BNP, RG 84, Vol. 57, File BU299-1, pt. 1.

78. LAC, Maxwell Graham to Commissioner, 16 Oct. 1919, Parks Canada Files, BNP, RG 84, Vol. 53, File BU232, pt. 1.

79. LAC, A. G. Smith recalled that while steers slaughtered up to the age of four years were in better condition than bulls of the same age, after four years their appearance and the quality of their hides were not good as bulls. A. G. Smith to the Controller, 15 Mar. 1939, Parks Canada Files, BNP, RG 84, Vol. 54, File BU232, pt. 5.

80. LAC, Commissioner to J. B. Harkin, 6 Sep. 1932, Parks Canada Files, BNP, RG 84, Vol. 54, File BU232, pt. 4.

81. LAC, James Smart to J. B. Harkin, 21 Apr. 1926, Parks Canada Files, BNP, RG 84, Vol. 53, File BU232, pt. 3.

82. LAC, J. B. Harkin to R. A. Gibson, 19 Apr. 1924, Parks Canada Files, BNP, RG 84, Vol. 57, File BU299-1, pt. 1.

83. LAC, J. B. Harkin to A. G. Smith, 19 Dec. 1922, Parks Canada Files, BNP, RG 84, Vol. 57, File BU299-1, pt. 1.

84. LAC, Maxwell Graham to J. B. Harkin, 29 Sept. 1919, Parks Canada Files, BNP, RG 84, Vol. 53, File BU232, pt. 1.

85. LAC, H. E. Sibbald to J. B. Harkin, 17 Jan. 1923, Parks Canada Files, BNP, RG 84, Vol. 52, File BU232-1, pt. 1.

86. LAC, Commissioner to H. E. Sibbald, 23 Jan. 1923, Parks Canada Files, BNP, RG 84, Vol. 52, File BU232-1, pt. 1.

87. LAC, Memorandum to W. W. Cory, 31 Aug. 1925, Parks Canada Files, BNP, RG 84, Vol. 57, File BU299-1, pt. 1.

88. LAC, Memorandum to W. W. Cory, 31 Aug. 1925, Parks Canada Files, BNP, RG 84, Vol. 57, File BU299-1, pt. 1.

89. LAC, Memorandum from C. E. Nagle, 19 Dec. 1924, Memorandum to Mr. Graham, 10 Jan. 1925 and Commissioner to S. J. Hungerford, 3 Mar. 1925, Parks Canada Files, BNP, RG 84, Vol. 52, File BU232-1, pt. 1.

90. It was estimated that for 2,000 head it would cost the department $6,000 to dispose of the bison by tender on the hoof and approximately $24,000 for the department to conduct an internal slaughter. With the latter option, the department questioned whether the sale of the bison products would raise enough revenue to offset the cost. LAC, C. Nagle to Mr. Bateman, 30 Nov. 1925, Parks Canada Files, BNP, RG 84, Vol. 53, File BU232, pt. 3. Sending the bison north, from a financial point of view, was the most logical plan, especially since the department had already invested in the infrastructure to corral and load the bison in 1925.

91. LAC, Commissioner to Geo. B. Grinnell, 21 Apr. 1925, Parks Canada Files, BNP, RG 84, Vol. 53, File BU232, pt. 3.

92. LAC, Commissioner to Lewis Freeman, 14 Nov. 1927, Parks Canada Files, BNP, RG 84, Vol. 52, File BU232-1, pt. 2.

93. LAC, O. S. Finnie to J. B. Harkin 27 Apr. 1925, Parks Canada Files, BNP, RG 84, Vol. 52, File BU232-1, pt. 1; LAC, Memorandum to O. S. Finnie, 29 Jul. 1925 and A. G. Smith to J. C. Hargrave, 25 Jun. 1925, Parks Canada Files, BNP, RG 84, File BU232-1, pt. 2; and LAC, *Edmonton Journal*, 13 Jun. 1925, "150 Bison Branded in One Day's Work," Parks Canada Files, BNP, RG 84, Vol. 53, File BU232-1, pt. 3.

94. LAC, Letter to W. W. Cory, 16 Jul. 1925, Parks Canada Files, BNP, RG 84, Vol. 52, File BU232-1, pt. 2.

95. Ray Sharp, interviewer unknown, circa 2001, VHS, Buffalo National Park Foundation Archives, (hereafter BNPFA), Wainwright, AB.

96. LAC, *Edmonton Journal*, 15 Jun. 1925, "Cowboys Win in Tug-O-War with 800-Pound Buffalo; Load Cars at Wainwright," Parks Canada Files, BNP, RG 84, Vol. 53, File BU232-1, pt. 3.

97. LAC, A. G. Smith to J. B. Harkin, 3 May 1926, Parks Canada Files, BNP, RG 84, Vol. 52, File BU232-1, pt. 2.

98. At that time, the park had around 8,500 bison. LAC, A. G. Smith to Commissioner, 30 Apr. 1926, Parks Canada Files, BNP, RG 84, Vol. 52, File BU232-1, pt. 2.

99. LAC, Letter to Hon. T. G. Murphy, 3 Nov. 1933, John Burns to J. B. Harkin, 28 Oct. 1933, and R. S. Munn to A. G. Smith, 6 Jun. 1933, Parks Canada Files, BNP, RG 84, Vol. 57, File BU299, pt. 9.

100. LAC, J. B. Harkin to Messrs. Gainers Limited, 22 Jun. 1933, Parks Canada Files, BNP, RG 84, Vol. 57, File BU299, pt. 9.

101. LAC, Harkin to Messrs. Burns & Company and Letter to H. H. Rowatt, 28 Oct. 1933, Parks Canada Files, BNP, RG 84, Vol. 57, File BU299, pt. 9.

102. LAC, Burns & Co. Ltd. to J. B. Harkin, 5 Nov. 1935 and J. B. Harkin to Messrs. Burns & Company Ltd., 20 Nov. 1935, Parks Canada Files, BNP, RG 84, Vol. 58, File BU299, pt. 11.

103. LAC, Burns and Co. Limited to F. H. H. Williamson, 9 Feb. 1939, Parks Canada Files, BNP, RG 84, Vol. 58, File BU299, pt. 14.

104. LAC, J. B. Harkin to Colin C. Moncrieff, 15 Dec. 1922, Parks Canada Files, BNP, RG 84, Vol. 52, File BU232-1, pt. 1.

CHAPTER FOUR

Zookeepers and Animal Breeders

Overpopulation, Range Degradation, and Disease,
1920–1939

BY THE 1930S, NATIONAL PARKS HAD COME TO BE DEFINED by their roles as reserves for wild animals. In 1933, J. B. Harkin, commissioner of the Parks Branch from 1911 until 1936, stated, "animal Parks fulfil two objects; the primary object is as breeding grounds, and the secondary object is as exhibition places."[1] Thus, national parks, as reserves for wild animals, functioned in two simultaneous roles: as zoos and as breeding grounds. In Rocky Mountains Park, animals were displayed in the paddock and the zoo to draw tourists, but the game in the park was also encouraged to breed so that the surplus would spill outside the borders to furnish the adjacent area for sportsmen.

While Buffalo National Park attempted to fulfill this dual role, it never accomplished this successfully. Rather, the park came to be defined by the problems it faced. The park's overpopulation peaked in 1925–26 and again reached dangerous levels in the early 1930s. While the other animal populations, in particular the deer but also the elk and moose, were also increasing, these animals were considered game species.[2] Measures were taken to reduce the bison herd, but any notion of reducing the other game populations provoked public criticism. The pressure of overgrown animal populations led to the degradation of the range and also contributed to the decline in the bison herd's health and the spread of disease, of which tuberculosis was the most serious. Consequently, the main impetus of Buffalo National Park, from the 1920s to its closure, was crisis management.

Several investigations of the park were carried out by various experts from 1923 until the park's closure. The common theme of all these reports was that the condition of the park would not improve unless the bison herd was reduced and new range was secured. Hampered by financial constraints, however, the Parks Branch was never able to reduce the herd effectively and could not carry out the major recommendations made by the experts. By the

1930s, the conditions of the park had not improved and the incidence of disease was on the rise among the animal populations. These were leading factors in the decision to close the park in 1939.

Howard Douglas, the second superintendent of Rocky Mountains Park, realized early on that tourists were drawn to the national parks to see animal life. He began his experiment of displaying wild animals to the public at Rocky Mountains Park by importing plains bison,[3] mountain sheep, angora goats, elk, mule deer, and moose.[4] He built a display paddock, which was later expanded to two hundred hectares. In 1907, however, he opened a zoo in Banff town site and some of the animals were moved to this new location.[5] Sid Marty argues that the experiment of the zoo made these animals even more accessible to tourists and proved "pivotal in changing the attitudes on wildlife preservation in the national parks. For the first time…[wild animals] were seen as an asset, and a potentially valuable one, as a source of interest to tourists."[6] Exhibiting wildlife proved to be a financially successful venture. Janet Foster notes that the Deputy Minister of the Interior, the minister who oversaw the early national parks, was pleased with the success of the animal preserve. By 1905, the revenue in Rocky Mountains Park "more than doubled the amount required for expenditure and maintenance."[7]

Given that Howard Douglas was heavily involved in the purchase of the animals for Buffalo National Park and acted as commissioner from 1908 to 1911,[8] it should not be surprising that the park followed a pattern almost identical to that of Rocky Mountains Park. As early as 1910, elk, moose, and pronghorn antelope were purchased for Buffalo National Park.[9] In fact, some of the first elk were purchased from Michel Pablo: seven elk, two bucks and five does were transported to the park in May 1911.[10] While mule deer would become the most prolific game animal in the park, they were indigenous to the area and became part of the park when the fence was built.[11] At this time, two pronghorn antelope bucks were also enclosed inside the park.[12]

Overhunting had severely reduced pronghorn antelope numbers by the early 20th century and in the first years of the tenure of Commissioner J. B. Harkin, parks were set aside in Alberta and Saskatchewan to protect the species. Three of these areas later became national parks.[13] Four years earlier, however, Buffalo National Park had been charged with the responsibility of saving the antelope. In 1910, Douglas commissioned C. J. Blazier to capture antelope to raise in the national parks because he feared that "in a very few years these animals will be extinct in Alberta and there are no others in any part of Canada."[14] Of the thirteen captured by Blazier, nine were delivered to Buffalo Park and four to Rocky Mountains Park.[15]

Like Rocky Mountains Park, the northeastern corner of Buffalo National Park was essentially a menagerie, designated to display different species of animals. This Visitor's Park comprised two enclosures, one known as the Small Buffalo Park and an even smaller enclosure at Mott Lake, which was also a recreational ground.[16] On an early Buffalo National Park map, the area was labelled as an "Enclosure for Elk, Moose, Antelope and a few Buffalo."[17] As with Banff, there were also exotic animals displayed in the Visitor's Park. In 1921, eleven male and eight female yak were shipped from Rocky Mountains Park for an exhibition herd.[18] Warden Ray Sharp remembered, "They had about 100 head of buffalo and maybe 150 head of elk in there for people to visit from town. And also yak and some of the cattalo."[19] Clearly influenced by the successful experiment of displaying animals in Rocky Mountains Park, the Visitor's Park was placed in close proximity to the town of Wainwright and the railway to attract visitors to the park.

The Visitor's Park fulfilled its role and attracted many tourists to the park. In May 1918, the Buffalo National Park annual report stated that "about 5,000 visitors from all parts of the continent registered during the year."[20] Furthermore, the *Edmonton Bulletin* stated that while the total number of visitors numbered around 6,000 in the mid-1920s, in 1929, 18,753 visitors registered at the park, and that number was believed to be low given that many visitors did not register. It also reported that on one single day of 1929, 400 motor cars entered the park carrying approximately 1,500 visitors.[21] Diary entries from 1929 by Davey Davison, warden and keeper of the north gate of the park, substantiate the high volume of tourists at the park. Visitors registered from all over Canada and the United States, England, Germany, and Australia. In the summer months Davison, or one of his family members, toured visitors through the park on a daily basis. On some days, the volume of visitors was quite high. On June 12, a party of 240 Shriners from Charlotte, South Carolina, toured the park. On July 23 and July 24, Davison mentions the park gate registered four pages of visitors.[22]

While the animals in the Visitor's Park succeeded in attracting visitors, their confinement to a small area and the actions of visitors with good intentions often contributed to the decline in the health of the animals. Specifically, the pronghorn antelope, primarily raised in the Home Paddock, did not fare well in captivity and continued to die from unknown causes and accidents. One of their more common ailments was a condition that involved ulcers on the neck or the jaw. This condition was first noticed in Banff in 1910, when two antelope died from ulcers that appeared on their necks.[23] At that time, A. B. Macdonald, superintendent of Rocky Mountains Park, determined that the condition was due to climate. He believed that the environment of the mountains was not suitable for this prairie species and in 1911 decided to send three of the remaining four animals in Rocky Mountains Park, all of which had evidence of ulcers, to Wainwright.[24] However, the antelope continued to suffer in their new location. Of the nine antelope delivered to Buffalo National Park in 1910, six died. Four more were shipped from Rocky Mountains Park, bringing the total to seven, but three of these died during 1911–12.[25] High mortality among the antelope was a trend that continued throughout the park's existence.

While the cause of the antelope mortality at Buffalo National Park was unknown, Howard Douglas suspected the lack of some type of weed or brush that they needed for a healthy diet. However, he also believed their deaths could be attributed to the fact they were kept in captivity to protect them from coyotes. Because they were on the verge of extinction, Douglas felt it was necessary to keep them confined for one year, until they were big enough to protect themselves from coyotes, and then turn them out into the main park where they could get the feed they required.[26]

Years later, Edgar McHugh, superintendent of Nemiskam Antelope Park in southern Alberta, which was established in 1915, commented on the disease to Harkin. McHugh was familiar with the symptoms and believed it to be an ailment of tame antelope confined to small enclosures. He described the symptoms as a lump on the jaw that contained a yellowish discharge. He believed the disease to be contagious and fatal, stating, "I have never known one to recover."[27] In his opinion, the ailment resulted from a lack of subsistence food, such as alkali, sage brush, and certain varieties of short grass. He felt it absolutely necessary that antelope have access to sagebrush.[28] S. E. Clarke, Department of Agriculture agrostologist, and Frank Shutt, Dominion chemist, concurred with McHugh that certain forage types, specifically sage bush and mosses, were important to the health of antelope.[29]

The antelopes' confinement may have contributed to their ailment. Warden Bud Cotton believed that the high mortality of the antelope resulted from tourists overfeeding them:

The use of hounds was found to be the most effective way to control the coyote population in Buffalo National Park. Herb Dixon tells how his grandfather Herb Walker, park farm superintendent, used a democrat or a sleigh to hunt coyotes. His fox terrier sat up front with him and a greyhound and Irish and Russian wolfhounds were kept in the box on the back. When the fox terrier spotted a coyote, he would start barking, try to run after it and the hounds were released from the box. The greyhound would overtake the coyote and grab one of its hind legs and flip it over. This would happen several times, slowing down the chase until the wolfhounds could catch up. The hounds were trained to hold the coyote and not tear the hide until Walker arrived to kill the coyote. He carried a small revolver or .22 calibre rifle for that purpose.

Later other antelope were shipped in. These were kept in a small, fenced pasture so that the tourists could take pictures of them. They were real tame and would come up for offerings of oats. But they, too, died. I attribute their demise to misplaced human kindness. Some days when the tourist season was at its peak, these antelope got about a gallon or more of oats each. Grain fed to any wild animal will eventually kill it.[30]

Buffalo National Park never successfully established a viable herd of antelope.

While the exhibition areas were an important place for displaying the animals to draw tourists, parks were also deemed important for propagating game species. In 1921, C. Gordon Hewitt, Dominion entomologist, wrote that this was one of the great advantages of the mountain reserves: "[Rocky Mountains Park], together with Jasper and Waterton Lakes Parks, will serve as unrivalled breeding-grounds for the big-game animals of the Rocky Mountains region, and the surplus wild-life population will afford a constant supply of big-game and fur-bearing animals for the adjacent unprotected regions."[31] By supplying areas with game, the national parks were providing a service that benefited both the parks system and the country as a whole.

With the exception of the pronghorn antelope, Buffalo National Park proved very successful as a breeding ground for the bison and other animals. In fact, it was too successful for its own good. As a prairie park, Buffalo National Park could not replicate the propagation scheme of Rocky Mountains Park's entirely. In the mountain parks, surplus game could spill outside the borders and occupy adjacent regions, furnishing the area for sportsmen. Buffalo National Park, however, was a prairie park in the middle of a settled area. It was never intended that the bison be released and the other animals did not move freely outside the park borders. By the 1920s, Buffalo National Park was experiencing a population crisis. The bison population was at its highest in 1925–26 with 8,832 animals. The other game populations were certainly not as large as the bison herd, but their numbers added additional pressure to the park. The total population was actually 10,528, more than twice the park's recommended carrying capacity, which was estimated in 1931 to be 5,000 head[32](see Table 4). The overgrown animal populations taxed the resources of the range and created ideal conditions for the spread of disease.

The addition of other game species to the bison preservation effort was not the only factor that contributed to the overpopulation problem. Eliminating coyotes in Buffalo National Park also contributed to overpopulation.

TABLE 4: WILDLIFE POPULATIONS IN BUFFALO NATIONAL PARK, 1922–32					
Year	*Bison*	*Moose*	*Elk*	*Deer*	*Total*
1922–23	6,780	28	218	-	-
1923–24	6,655	29	288	1,194	8,136
1924–25	8,267	30	290	1,173	9,760
1925–26	8,832	35	368	1,293	10,528
1926–27	6,026	48	400	1,486	7,960
1927–28	4,241	54	472	1,653	6,420
1928–29	4,300	60	565	1,824	6,749
1929–30	5,016	66	654	1,994	7,730
1930–31	6,231	76	766	2,172	9,245
1931–32	6,331	86	916	2,500	9,833

Source: LAC, Memorandum to J. B. Harkin, 15 Feb. 1933, Parks Canada Files, BNP, RG 84, Vol. 50, BU217, pt. 1.

Coyotes, classified as predators, were controlled because they posed a threat to the growth of the animal populations inside the reserve. Not until the 1930s did the national parks system recognize that these predators were essential to maintaining a balanced ecosystem. Rather, coyotes were blamed for the deaths of wild animals and birds, but they were also considered a menace because they destroyed heads and hides that were otherwise profitable when sold.[33] As early as 1913, Park Superintendent William McTaggart noted how plentiful coyotes were in the park and said that he was going to have "all the riders carry rifles on the round up with an endeavour to slaughter as many of them as possible."[34]

Coyotes were also killed in Buffalo National Park because of pressure from settlers outside the park, especially those who had property adjacent to its borders. Annie Armstrong, a settler from the Fabyan area whose property was bordered by the park's page wire fence on two sides, complained that coyotes had eaten chickens, eggs, and a pig, and were posing a threat to small calves. These were revenue sources that she and other settlers could not afford to lose. While people who lived farther away from the park were able to kill the coyotes, she could not: "here where we are right against the 'Coyote Reserve' of 100,000 acres, in which shooting is not allowed, the wolves[35] have learned to come out and help them selves to the poultry and dash back in again." She continued, "Now, with this Park, I look upon the Dominion Government as a neighbor of mine who is not being neighborly, when such nuisances are protected to my detriment."[36] The fact that coyotes recognized the park as a safe haven was confirmed by Bernard Hervey, chief superintendent of Dominion Parks in 1916. He stated, "As matters now stand when the coyotes are hunted outside they at once make a break for the Park, [jump] through the fence and leisurely stroll inside knowing that they are perfectly safe."[37]

For these reasons, the Parks Branch initiated a campaign to control the coyote population in the park. Because the park consisted of mostly open country, hounds were used to hunt coyotes as it was believed to be the most efficient method. The campaign was very successful. Maxwell Graham reported that in the 1917–18 fiscal year, 65 coyotes were destroyed, over three times the number that had been killed in the previous season. In fact, he considered the use of hounds to eliminate coyotes so efficient that he suggested that trained hounds be used in Jasper, Rocky Mountains, and Waterton Lakes to rid these national parks of predators (see Table 5).[38]

TABLE 5: CENSUS OF COYOTES KILLED UNDER HOUND CAMPAIGN IN BUFFALO NATIONAL PARK, 1917–28		
Year	Killed by Hounds	Total Killed
1917–18	53	65
1918–19	81	83
1919–20	49	52
1920–21	50	59
1921–22	61	65
1922–23	46	51
1923–24	47	56
1924–25	57	67
1925–26	44	48
1926–27	96	118
1927–28	45	65

Source: LAC, Parks Canada Files, BNP, RG 84, Vol. 55, File BU262, pt. 1.

In the first years of the campaign, owners with hounds were authorized to hunt coyotes under the supervision of park riders.[39] However, in the winter of 1918, A. G. Smith suggested, and Harkin approved, that Foreman Herb Walker and Caretaker Dave Davison, who had their own hounds, control the coyote population instead of enlisting private individuals. The men were allowed to keep the hides of the coyotes they killed in payment for the use of their dogs, feed, and any possible loss, Given that hides were worth about three to five dollars each, the incentive was likely somewhat responsible for the high number of coyotes killed over the next ten years.[40] In fact, the business of eliminating this predator was quite lucrative for park employees. In 1926–27, 118 coyotes were killed. Of the 84 hides that were marketed, employees were averaging at least eight dollars per coyote skin (see Table 6).

In 1928, however, it was decided at the superintendents' conference that wardens would no longer be allowed to keep furs from any animals trapped in the park.[41] After this decision was made, not as many coyotes were killed, although part of the reason was that there were not as many left to hunt. Not until 1934 did coyote numbers increase again to a point where Superintendent Smith believed it was necessary to begin controlling the population again.[42] However, even in 1935, when the national parks policy changed and predators began to be recognized as an integral part of the ecosystem, Smith thought that in the case of Buffalo National Park this new policy should not be strictly followed. He argued that because the bison were enclosed inside the park they were at the mercy of the coyote. Furthermore, protecting the coyotes would invite trouble from those settled outside the park borders. Instead, Smith advised that a modified coyote population control should go on[43] and coyotes continued to be hunted throughout the park's existence.

The designation of the other animal populations in Buffalo National Park as game species was another important factor contributing to the park's overpopulation crisis. Although bison had been slaughtered since 1922 to reduce their population, the status of other animals as game impeded the department's effort to devise an appropriate solution for reducing their numbers. Except for 311 elk in 1938,[44] none of the other game animals were slaughtered until the closure of the park in 1940. In the case of the surplus deer, for example, most Alberta sportsmen were against controlling this population through slaughter but thought every effort should be made to distribute the surplus deer to benefit sport hunting.[45] George Spargo, secretary of the Alberta Fish and Game Association, relayed the argument they used; "what is the object of having a concentration of big game within the confines

TABLE 6: SALE OF COYOTE SKINS BY PARK EMPLOYEES, 1926–27				
Hunted By	Total Killed	No Value	Marketed	Amount Received
H. B. Walker	52	6	46	$556.00
E. J. Cotton	13	1	12	$99.00
D. W. Davison	43	27	16	$140.00
H. F. Dunning	10	-	10	$100.00
Total	118	34	84	$895.00

Source: NAC, A. G. Smith to J. B. Harkin, 25 Apr. 1927, Parks Canada Files, BNP, RG 84, Vol. 55, File BU262, pt. 1.

of the National Parks if it isn't to increase 'Big Game'...if we are going to shoot the natural increase of what avail is it in keeping these huge tracts of land?...They [sportsmen] state that every effort should be made to have such a surplus distributed so that sport will benefit."[46]

The sensitivity of the issue of slaughtering the park's game population is perhaps best illustrated by the various attempts to reduce the mule deer population. Next to the bison, deer were the most prolific species in the park. Concern over the mule deer population first surfaced in 1923. Dr. Seymour Hadwen, pathologist with the Department of Agriculture, found in his investigation of the park that mule deer were almost as numerous as the bison and believed to be eating up much of their food. He recommended that their numbers be reduced.[47] While the Parks Branch initially wished to slaughter the animals as it had the bison, they never took this avenue.[48] Clearly, their status as game was already an issue by 1923 given that J. B. Harkin consulted Benjamin Lawton, the chief game guardian of the province of Alberta, for his opinion on how the department could best dispose of the deer. Lawton suggested three options: sportsmen could be given an opportunity to shoot the deer, they could be slaughtered in the same manner as the bison and the meat used as a food supply, or they could be turned loose outside the park.[49] A decade later, it appears no action had yet been taken to reduce the herd. The recommendations of S. H. Clark, Game Commissioner in 1932, were solutions that would have certainly been more palatable to sport hunters. He recommended that the deer could be liberated out of the west side of the park into the Battle River Valley, shipped by rail to the foothills to stock this area, or slaughtered and the meat donated to charitable organizations. Clark's first two recommendations would have fulfilled one of the mandates of the early national parks system: to furnish game to areas outside park borders. However, the areas outside Buffalo National Park were settled farmland rather than hunting territory. Clark's third recommendation appears to have been offered as a last resort; he did not support slaughtering the deer at this time as he believed there would be considerable reaction if the first two recommendations were not tried first.[50] The fact that deer were never slaughtered until the park's closure suggests that this alternative was never deemed acceptable.

Because the department knew that the slaughter of game animals would provoke criticism, they explored other avenues of downsizing these animal populations. The department attempted, with some success, to ship game to other areas in Canada.[51] Shipping costs, however, made the venture very expensive. Game commissioners Bryan Williams from British Columbia and A. E. Etter of Saskatchewan were both interested in the offer of elk, but the cost of shipping proved to be the biggest roadblock. While Williams was able to take one carload of the animals to British Columbia because the railway granted them free passage, the Canadian National Railway did not grant Etter free transportation. Since he could not raise the necessary funds to transport the elk, he was unable to save any animals.[52]

While elk could be successfully shipped, the temperament of the mule deer made transportation of these animals problematic. Although there was interest in acquiring deer to stock other areas, Benjamin Lawton, in 1923, was concerned about shipping them. He stated, "I am personally afraid that the loss due to accidents in corralling, loading, shipping and unloading might be sufficient to offset the good that might be done."[53] Moreover, transporting deer was more expensive than shipping other game. Although elk could be shipped without crating inside a rail car that would hold up to twenty-five head,[54] deer were more nervous and prone to injury. Each deer had to be transported inside a crate and they often died from shock during transport or shortly after arriving at a new location.[55] As a consequence, the Parks Branch never attempted to ship deer.

Trials to liberate the mule deer, considered the best solution for reducing this animal population by the Alberta Fish and Game Association,[56] started in 1933. The park decided to release deer out the west gate into the Battle River Valley. However, several problems with this plan soon surfaced. In 1933, Harkin believed that the park needed to reduce the deer population by 1,500 animals.[57] However, S. H. Clark, Game Commissioner of Alberta, thought no more than 300 deer should be released into the Battle River area.[58] Furthermore, even though the plan was to liberate the deer into an area adjacent to the park, the animals were not easily driven and the Parks Branch soon realized that the effort and labour involved in releasing the deer were going to be costly. In an attempt to offset some of the cost, J. B. Harkin wrote Clark for help. Using the argument that the deer would be a benefit to the province of Alberta, Harkin asked Clark if the province could pay one dollar per deer, for up to 300 deer, towards the cost of releasing them.[59] But Clark responded that the provincial Game Branch was not in a position, nor did it feel obligated, to put any money towards the proposal.[60]

Initially, the Parks Branch decided to absorb the cost of releasing the deer because it wanted to insure that the province would take more excess deer in the future.[61] Its method of doing so, however, showed that it lacked the financial will to follow through on the scheme. Park personnel in Wainwright decided to capture deer in the horse pasture at Rocky Ford, an area in the west side of the park. This method involved minimal labour since they enticed the animals into the pasture with salt licks and oat sheaves. Although the low fence proved unable to contain the deer, they fixed this initial glitch by installing a high wire fence.[62] In 1935, they released 53 deer and A. G. Smith believed that this method could be a means by which a number of deer could be turned out each winter.[63]

The scheme was never successful enough, however, in reducing the deer herd numbers significantly. Although the park needed to reduce the deer populations in 1933, deliberations over the best and most cost-effective method meant none were released until 1935. In that year, the 53 deer that had gathered in the pen were substantially fewer than the 300 animals allowed by the province. Due to the deep snow in 1936, which localized the deer population in the bush, the park was able to trap and release only 27 deer.[64] Considering that the park needed to reduce the deer herd by at least 1,500 animals, such a small number did not result in any significant change. Furthermore, the purpose behind releasing the deer, to restock the Battle River area, was precluded when most of the deer released the first winter were shot illegally.[65]

The controversy surrounding the culling of the game in Buffalo National Park resulted in virtually no reduction of the deer, elk, and moose populations during the park years. When added to the overpopulated bison herd, these other animals contributed to the range crisis in the park. Officials were concerned with the affect this overpopulation was having on the conditions of the range and the health of the animals.

J. B. Harkin hired experts to investigate and make recommendations on how to improve conditions at the park. The first major investigation of the park took place in 1923. Dr. Seymour Hadwen, pathologist with the Department of Agriculture, with the assistance of A. E. Cameron, animal pathologist for the veterinary director general from Lethbridge and Dr. Christian, the meat inspector in charge of the slaughter from the Meat and Canned Foods Division, Edmonton, reported on the health of the animals, their management, and the condition of the range.

Hadwen spent over two weeks at Buffalo National Park in January and February of 1923. His report revealed the park was in a serious crisis. Of the herd Hadwen wrote, "The condition of the animals could not be called good." He took several drives around the park with Foreman Herb Walker and did not see any considerable amount of forage cover and noticed the animals were eating browse and small twigs. This fact was confirmed on the killing floor during the cull that winter: "we found that their paunches were filled with willow twigs and browse, with the exception of those which were eating hay."[66]

Hadwen classified the range as overgrazed. Ribs showed on most of the animals, proof that the lack of forage was affecting their health.[67] Although he believed the range might recover to some extent if the upcoming season was wet, he warned that many of the animals had grazed the grasses and plants so short that they could not produce seed. He recommended that park officials secure new range to allow the present range to recuperate and reduce the bison herd greatly. He also thought a study of the range was needed to determine its carrying capacity and how long it would take to return it to its original state.[68]

Hadwen also found that the overpopulated state of the park contributed to the spread of disease among the animal populations. Several parasites, of which *Fascioloides magna*, or liver fluke, was one of the more serious, were discovered in the bison herd during the first cull at the park in the winter of 1922–23. Liver fluke caused injury in five to ten per cent of all the livers examined.[69] The most serious disease encountered in the slaughter, however, was tuberculosis.

In 1922–23 cull, the high incidence of tuberculosis found among the bison at Buffalo National Park was staggering. Seventy-five per cent, or 195 of 259 bison killed, were found to be affected.[70] The percentage was so high that Hadwen thought the whole herd should be considered as suffering from the disease.[71] Dr. Frederick Torrance, Veterinary Director General, reported to J. B. Harkin on information he received from inspector A. E. Cameron's report. He compared the figures from the 1922–23 bison cull at Buffalo National Park with the statistics for cattle killed at Canadian Abattoirs from 1 April to 30 November 1922 (see Table 7) and concluded: "These are most startling figures and indicate that the buffalo at Wainwright are very seriously affected with this disease, in fact the herd must be considered so badly affected that the eradication of tuberculosis from it is a hopeless proposition."[72]

While it is not known how this disease spread to the herd, one theory is that it arrived with bison that were imported from the Rocky Mountains Park herd during the purchase years. The disease first surfaced in the national park system in 1910, when Maxwell Graham reported that five bison died from it in Canadian parks. The only parks that kept bison at that time were Rocky Mountains Park, Elk Island Reserve, and Buffalo Park Reserve.[73]

TABLE 7: COMPARISON OF FIGURES FROM 1923–24 BISON CULL AT BUFFALO NATIONAL PARK AND FIGURES FOR CATTLE KILLED AT CANADIAN ABATTOIRS FROM APRIL 1 – NOVEMBER 30, 1922					
Buffalo killed	*No. affected Tuberculosis*	*Percentage*	*Carcases condemned*	*Percentage of affected*	*Percentage of killed*
259	199	76.83	60	30.15	23.16
Figures for cattle killed at Canadian Abattoirs: (April 1 to Nov. 30 1922)					
379,857	24,422	6.44	4,028	16.48	1.23

Source: LAC, Frederick Torrance to J.B. Harkin, 27 Mar. 1923, Parks Canada Files, BNP, RG 84, Vol. 58, File BU299-2, pt. 1.

The first case of tuberculosis in Buffalo National Park was discovered in the post-mortem of a bison bull on 20 December 1916.[74] Following this discovery, tuberculosis was suspected in many of the bison that exhibited enlarged joints.[75] Since no tuberculosis was confirmed in Buffalo National Park until 1916 and the Elk Island herd was free from the disease, it is likely that the five animals that died of tuberculosis were from the Banff herd.[76]

If the source was the Banff herd, one or both of the shipments of bison that came from that park could have infected the Wainwright herd. Seventy-seven bison were transferred from Rocky Mountains Park to Wainwright on 31 October 1909 and ten on 31 March 1914.[77] However, it is unlikely that this was the source of the disease. During the first Montana shipment to Elk Island Reserve, one car of bison bulls and cows was shipped to Rocky Mountains Park in exchange for a carload from this park with an equal number of bison from that herd to go to Elk Island Reserve. Even after this shipment from Rocky Mountains Park, the Elk Island herd remained virtually disease-free.

Other theories were that the herd was exposed to the disease before it was moved to Canada or that the source could have been spread through the milk supply.[78] During the 1922–23 slaughter, Hadwen noted that "[i]n a number of cases the disease had been arrested and the glands showed a state of calcification, or hardening, which is an indication that the disease is not active."[79] It was the general opinion of officials in the Department of Agriculture that the Pablo bison were exposed to tuberculosis in Montana when they were pastured on the open range with cattle.[80]

If the herd was exposed to tuberculosis prior to arriving in Wainwright, it may explain how it became infected so quickly and extensively. The over-populated conditions and poor range at Buffalo National Park, however, were certainly conducive to the spread of disease. Tuberculosis likely spread through the herd by all the conventional ways in which it was known to spread—by inhalation, through the digestive tract by consumption of milk or other contaminated food, during breeding season, and from a mother to her unborn calf.[81] Torrance believed the overcrowded conditions of the range, which resulted in a scarcity of feed, also contributed to the spread of disease among the bison. He considered the manner in which they were fed, however, as the biggest contributing factor. "…the hay is spread out upon the same ground day after day. This ground becomes contaminated from the droppings of the buffalo, the hay becomes soiled and readily carries infection to fresh victims."[82]

Some officials in the Parks Branch were concerned about the spread of disease even before the incidence of tuberculosis was known. In 1916, Maxwell Graham was concerned about the overcrowded conditions of the range and its relation to the spread of disease. He noted, "The number of bison today in Buffalo Park amount to nearly 1700. Whatever danger of an outbreak of contagious disease there might have been in the past, when their number was smaller, is today vastly increased. Such danger becomes increasingly acute during the winter months, as it is then that the animals are confined and restricted."[83] However, on the whole, the tubercular state of the bison herd was treated in a passive manner. Part of the reason for this lack of concern was the way in which evidence of tuberculosis was interpreted following the 1923 slaughter. While Hadwen argued that the entire herd should be considered tubercular, he was surprised to find the bison in such good condition: "Taking the herd as a whole (ante mortem), however, the disease does not show as markedly as one would expect. It is true that here and there one may see an emaciated coughing animal, but as a general thing the disease is not in great evidence."[84]

Following the slaughter, Harkin met with Department of Agriculture officials Dr. Torrance, Dr. Watson, Dr. Barnes, E. S. Archibald, and A. G. Smith to discuss the tuberculosis in the herd. In a memorandum to Deputy Minister W. W. Cory about the meeting, Harkin said that since the tuberculosis appeared arrested in many of the cases, the situation was not as serious as first thought. He informed Cory that although the high percentage of animals afflicted with tuberculosis was initially alarming, the calcified scars in the lungs of many of the older animals meant the disease was not active. "It was the general opinion that the animals were affected when they were first put in the Park, but the disease had not developed sufficiently to make it at all noticeable unless under special test or post-mortem examination."[85]

The commercial value of the bison seemed to trump any concern over the herd's diseased state. While it was impossible to eradicate the disease, Harkin stated the general opinion of these officials "was that the conditions were not serious enough to affect the utilization of the herd for commercial purposes." Harkin continued:

> Owing to the natural increase the herd has developed to the state where it was considered it could be of considerable economic value to the country. For the purely sentimental reasons only it is considered,

if possible, effort should be made to maintain a herd in the healthiest condition possible. This is important in connection with all cross-breeding and other experiments to be made with the buffalo.[86]

Another reason that the issue of tuberculosis was downplayed was that it was a taboo issue, and Harkin did not wish to publicize the high incidence of tuberculosis found among the bison. In April, Dr. E. A. Watson, chief pathologist, asked for permission to publish the finding of tuberculosis among the Wainwright herd, arguing it would be "somewhat misleading to publish our general findings as to pathological and parasitological conditions in our buffalo without mentioning the most extensive and important of them all, namely, tuberculosis. New observations on the epidemiology of tuberculosis must always be of value in the study of this problem and should be made available to all concerned in it."[87] An article by A. E. Cameron entitled "Notes on Buffalo: Anatomy, Pathological Conditions, and Parasites," which had been published in the *Veterinary Journal*, gave a detailed analysis of all the other ailments of the Wainwright bison, but gave no indication of the extent that tuberculosis was ravaging the herd.[88] However, even with Watson's suggestion that the findings should be published in a foreign journal that would not receive attention from the public, Harkin made it clear that he did not want anything published on the tuberculosis in the herd.[89] Consequently, in a subsequent article by Cameron, the presence of disease was downplayed and only one sentence near the end of the article alluded to it: "Tuberculosis has been found in the buffalo, as is common in wild animals in captivity."[90]

Nevertheless, the Parks Branch continued to be pressured to reveal that the herd was diseased. The Veterinary Director General of the Health of Animals Branch, while respecting the request of the Parks Branch not to publish the tuberculosis in the herd, felt that the existence of the disease could be admitted because it was well known. Even when the Parks Branch did begin to admit that the herd was diseased, as was apparent in a 1928 letter to the Saskatchewan Anti-Tuberculosis League, Harkin argued that the tuberculosis was decreasing and it was expected that it would gradually be eliminated.[91]

Investigators made several recommendations to aid in the recovery of the range and eliminate disease. Both Hadwen and Torrance recommended that the population of the herd be reduced, especially those in bad condition, and new range be secured to allow the existing range to recover. Since the whole bison herd was considered tubercular, Torrance did not see any practical way of picking out the small number of healthy ones from the diseased

In the winter, the bison herd was moved to quarters in the south part of the park. Traditionally, the herd was fed hay in the winter. During the drought years in the mid-1920s, however, wheat straw, which was purchased from local farmers, helped sustain the herd through the winter.

herd, except perhaps those less than one year old. While their methodology differed, both Torrance and Hadwen suggested a new bison herd be raised by separating calves from their mothers and placing them on new range. To further help reduce infection in the herd, they recommended the present herd be fed well and the feeding ground changed often. Hadwen believed the herd had to be put in better condition before it could be profitably slaughtered that upcoming fall.[92]

Based on this advice, J. B. Harkin made some recommendations in 1925. His first recommendation, that the herd be cut down by 2,000 head per year until they reached the grazing capacity of the park, was carried out but interrupted for a couple of years when bison were shipped north to Wood Buffalo National Park. However, it is not clear whether calves were separated to create the nucleus for a new healthy herd, and there is no evidence that animals were moved to new pastures. For the remainder of the decade the overpopulated bison herd and the problems associated with it continued to plague the park; lack of forage and disease continued to take their toll on the bison salvage effort.

While the size of the animal population in the park was the primary reason for the overgrazing, the deterioration of the range and spread of disease was also accelerated by environmental factors that park officials could not control. From 1916 to 1923, the time of the first investigations, the park had a series of dry years.[93] These conditions contributed to a lack of food available and forced park employees to feed the bison extra hay. Although the animals had been fed hay in the winter from the beginning of the effort,[94] the need to provide hay outside the winter season escalated as the herd increased in size and forage grew scarce. In 1923, Torrance noted in his report, "It has been shown that the range is much overcrowded, that feed becomes scarce, and the animals are, consequently, reduced in condition towards the close of the summer, and feeding of hay has to be carried out to supplement what they cannot obtain on the range."[95] Traditionally, Buffalo National Park also supplied other national parks with feed after it had reserved enough hay for its own needs, but the park was no longer in a position to provide food even for itself during the 1920s.[96]

During the mid-1920s, the park continued to be plagued by exceptionally dry years and harsh winters that destroyed vegetation and left the range severely damaged. In 1925, the Wainwright area experienced a prolonged winter. Superintendent Smith stated "This is the first winter we have noticed buffalo pawing snow like a horse, but that is the only way they can get through it, and they have eaten tons of willow brush."[97] The deep snow that year also meant that the range could not be grazed as early as usual.[98]

That same year, the Parks Branch decided to ship 2,000 bison north to Wood Buffalo Park to help reduce the population of the bison herd.[99] Although transporting bison out of Buffalo National Park was believed to be the most cost-effective means of reducing the herd and alleviating pressure on the range, the decision proved to be a tax on the park's food supply and placed an even greater financial strain on the park. After 1,179 bison had been segregated for the shipment north in January 1925, Superintendent A. G. Smith advised against rounding up any more in the spring because the cows were heavy at this time and he thought putting them through the corrals could cause serious damage to the herd. Furthermore, the animals already segregated in holding pens had to be fed extra feed. Because primarily younger bison were sent north, these animals were separated from their mothers earlier than otherwise necessary.[100] Smith stated, "Over 900 calves that, if they had not been separated, would have lived almost entirely on the cows, have since had to be fed daily."[101] He warned that if the Parks Branch wished to continue segregating additional animals for the shipment, the park would be out of feed in 30 to 40 days.[102] In addition, it took eleven park riders seventeen days to segregate the animals, and this cost had not been factored into the shipping estimate. Smith calculated that it would cost $1,323.20 to hire the extra riders and help, to round up the remainder of the bison to fill the shipment.[103]

The park did run out of hay as Smith predicted. In March, he wrote a desperate telegraph to Harkin and informed his superior that they needed more hay immediately.[104] Smith continued to be concerned over the feed supply that summer. Although they had the same number of bison to feed as in the previous year, the park possessed only half the amount of hay. He stated:

> You will, no doubt, recollect that we were obliged to purchase one hundred tons of baled hay last spring to carry us through…and we have been obliged to cut down in our feeding to insure having sufficient to carry us until the new hay is harvested.
>
> There is absolutely no upland or prairie wool hay in the park to cut and the slough hay on the Ribstone Meadow will not be fit to cut until about the end of this month.[105]

Later on in the summer, Warden Bud Cotton commented on the conditions of the range in his diary. On 13 August he wrote, "South in flats.

Range poor. With recent dry years and the overstocked condition of park, it will take years for the range to come back to its former condition." Two days later Cotton wrote, "Main herd drifting on flats and sand hills south of Elk Butte Range. In area covered today, devoid of grass, practically dried and eaten out. Looks bad for winter rustling for the buffalo."[106]

Drought and environmental factors continued to damage the range in the years following. In 1926–27, the park experienced its hardest winter since its establishment. Superintendent Smith reported that feed was already scarce as a result of fall frosts and heavy grazing.[107] The gravity of the situation climaxed when 256 bison perished. C. E. Nagle of the Parks Branch remarked that this high rate of mortality was neither unexpected nor avoidable: "The condition of the herd has been poor for the past three or four years as a result of over-grazing of the Park and severe winters."[108]

With snow pack and ice cover that year, employees at the park were forced to supplement the bison's feed with hay one month longer than usual. Once again, Smith had to purchase feed. However, because the park could not afford the better quality hay, he had to purchase the inferior wheat straw from local farmers.[109] He observed, "Large quantities of wheat straw were fed to the animals during the month and, although the animals, if in good condition, will exist on this class of fodder, they show the effects of the lack of sufficient feed of a more sustaining quality. I believe this fact accounts for the comparatively high rate of loss we sustained during this winter."[110] The 1927 diary kept by Warden Davey Davison, in which he reported on the activity of the North gate and Visitor parks, confirms these accounts. During these winter months, the park was reliant on oat and wheat straw and green feed from local farmers to feed to the animals in the paddocks. Nonetheless, several elk, and some deer and yak in the Visitor's Park died in the first few months of 1927.[111]

Even when precipitation improved in 1927, the superintendent noted, "I might say that owing to a larger fall of rain this season range conditions are improving some, but the effects of dry years when carrying too large a buffalo herd are still very evident."[112] Warden Cotton confirmed the effects that the lack of food was having on the herd. When segregating bison for shipment north in 1927, he described the "[a]nimals in semi-starved condition and hard to work as they go on the fight at the least provocation."[113] D. H. Christie of the North West Territories Branch echoed the same sentiments in a telegram to his director O. S. Finnie. He described the condition of the bison upon their arrival in Wood Buffalo Park that year as follows: "Buffalo in poor condition seemed to be starved."[114]

A herd of elk in Buffalo National Park. Photo William Carsell.

When Dr. S. E. Clarke, Assistant Agrostologist in the Department of Agriculture, made an investigation of the park in 1929, conditions had not improved. While he found the animals on the range appeared "to be in good thrifty condition, fairly well fleshed and free from disease and insects,"[115] overpopulation was continuing to take a toll on the range. His assessment echoed the earlier 1923 investigations. The inferiority of the range was not caused by lack of vegetation because it afforded "a wide selection of forage species, nearly all of which are quite palatable and highly nutritious."[116] Rather, the problem was that the summer range was subjected to continual grazing pressure from early spring to late fall. Clarke believed the physical features of the range also contributed to its depletion. While he noted there were many sloughs and several small lakes near the eastern boundary of the park, he reported "the south western part of the range is not so well watered. The lakes are very small and most of them dry up during dry seasons with the result that stock on these areas have to travel a long distance to water."[117]

Grazing in the early spring was especially detrimental because pressure on the range so early in the season did not allow the grass to develop properly. Trampling by the animals at this time of year destroyed seedlings and encouraged water run-off, which caused much of the deterioration. When grass was not permitted to develop, deep-rooted weeds of low forage value were able to take root. Clarke believed that excessive trampling and close grazing might have even prevented weed growth and resulted in soil erosion. While the range was free from poisonous plants, Clarke indicated that the forage was in its last stages:

> Prairie sage…that well known indicator of over grazing is very prevalent on nearly all parts of the range…The greater part of the summer range has been over-grazed and the pasture seriously depleted. This condition is most marked on the short grass areas adjacent to watering places…Many of the hillocks and ridges are grey with Prairie Sage (*Artemisia frigida*) and Club Moss (*Selaginella densa*) plants that are of little or no forage value, while the grasses have been almost entirely killed out. Such weeds are indicators of over-grazing and while they are of little forage value they do prevent soil drifting, they represent Nature's final attempt to cover up her nakedness. On large areas little or no seed of the more valuable forage species was produced during the summer of 1929, and very little will be produced as long as present grazing practices are followed, except it be during unusually wet seasons.[118]

Clarke made several recommendations to help improve the conditions of the range. First, as with the earlier 1923 assessments, he recommended that they acquire an alternate grazing area as soon as possible. The park already had an area the size of a township on the east side of the park, which had never been used. Clarke recommended that this area (the north half of township 42 and south half or township 43, range 5) be fenced for this purpose. He advised that they also acquire sections 7 to 12 in township 43, range 6 to connect this area to the main park.

Clarke also proposed that the summer range should be divided into a north and south section so a system of rotational grazing could be implemented that would allow pastures to recuperate. For a two-year period, the south field should be grazed in the spring and summer months allowing the north field to produce seed. The bison could graze on the north field in the fall after the plants have shed their seeds. After two years, the process would be reversed. The new area could be used as supplementary grazing for the spring and summer months. He also recommended more watering places be created in the west and south portions of the park, which would allow for more uniform grazing on the range. He believed officials should conduct reseeding experiments in overgrazed areas to see if this method would be a practical way of improving depleted pastures.[119]

Clarke again made an investigation in 1930. While his report mentioned that the bison, elk, and deer appeared in good condition, he was concerned that all these animals were increasing in number, which was causing the overgrazed condition of the pasture. The bison herd numbered around 5,000 head, but this would quickly increase with an estimated calf crop of 1,300. He believed that the park, which at one time could sustain 5,000 bison, could now sustain only 4,000 head[120] head of bison (of one year old and up). Since there had been no bison cull in 1930, he estimated that bison herd alone would approach 8,000 head with the calf crops of 1930 and 1931.[121]

In his assessment of the range, Clarke found there was little growth of early grasses due to lack of moisture, but rains, which started in mid-June, favoured later grasses and there was considerable secondary growth of the early grasses later in the summer and fall. Yet he still found evidence of overgrazing.

> Large areas on the upland pastures are grey with prairie sage (*Artemisia frigida*) and other patches are carpeted with Club-moss (*Selaginella densa*). These, along with other unpalatable weeds, are on the increase,

indicating an overgrazed condition and a general trend towards the perennial weed stage. Sand patches are increasing both in number and in size. The upland pastures had been grazed to a degree of 90% or over, while from 65 to 70% should be the maximum degree of grazing on this area for some years to come.[122]

Some of Clarke's smaller recommendations had been carried out from the previous year. A fence was moved to give the animals access to Ox-bow lake, connected with the Battle River, which provided slightly more pasture. Four sections and Boundary Lake, which contained good water, were in the process of being fenced to add to the winter quarters. Also, some reseeding tests were underway with different grasses, fescues, and clover. However, the summer range had not been subdivided and the unused grazing area on the east side of the park had not been fenced. Clarke did not believe it was wise to sub-divide the summer range unless park officials added new grazing area to the park and reduced the number of animals in the herd.[123]

If the Parks Branch could have acted upon the recommendations of the experts, they would have helped regenerate the range and reduce the incidence of disease. However, the Parks Branch was a small one in the Department of the Interior. Buffalo National Park's plight was not a priority to the Dominion government, especially during the Great Depression. The hands of those in the Parks Branch were tied and they did not have the power or the financial means to carry out any larger improvements. In 1933 Hoyes Lloyd, the Parks Branch ornithologist, stated, "Owing to lack of funds we will not be able to go on with the fencing this coming summer, and, therefore, the grazing area cannot be increased. And, so, the crowding and over-grazing will continue for at least this coming season. In the meantime, the range is going from bad to worse." He continued:

> As will be seen from the Schedule, there are some 9800 animals in Buffalo Park. There can be no doubt that this is far too great a burden for the grazing area. No opposing view has been expressed, either by those who have made scientific investigations or by the Superintendent. For one reason or another, however, we have been unable to act upon the outstanding recommendations. We sought advice, but were unable to apply the remedy.[124]

Clearly local park employees were concerned about the consequences that resulted from an overpopulated herd and their inability to act on the larger recommendations. In 1932, Superintendent Smith wrote:

The approximate area of our summer range is 71,680 acres including lakes, and during the coming season we shall have about 6200 buffalo one year old and up grazing on this pasture, which is less than 12 acres per animal…I think you will agree with me when I say that the over-grazed condition of our range will result in a herd of unhealthy and inferior animals. The change in the health of the herd, particularly the young animals, is evident in Inspector Waddy's report covering slaughter operations recently completed…The young animals in the herd to-day have not the rugged and healthy appearance of those the same age ten or fifteen years ago.[125]

In May of that same year Warden Cotton candidly reported, "Park range has been overstocked and grazed out for years. No amount of reseeding will do any good as long as animals remain in Park at their present numbers."[126]

As the Parks Branch was unable to follow through with any major recommendations, the crises did not improve. In the beginning of the 1930s, the animal populations were again approaching 10,000, the levels the park had experienced in the mid-1920s. The mule deer had also increased substantially (see Table 4).[127] While the deer overpopulation was alarming, Smith was actually more concerned about the increasing elk population competing with the bison for food. "It is known that elk do some browsing, but they graze mostly in the summer, and in winter they associate with the buffalo on the feed yards, if possible, which is something the deer never do."[128] In 1937, R. A. Gibson, director of Lands, Parks, and Forests Branch, reported that "the Elk…have increased in great number on account of protection, and are actually depleting the fodder supply to an extent where it is impossible to provide pasturage for the buffalo for which the Park was established, and which are the justification for its maintenance."[129]

Even more alarming, however, was the high rate of mortality among the deer population. In 1932, the deer population numbered 2,500 animals (see Table 4) and in February of that year, a number of deer and a few elk had been found dead or in a weakened state.[130] Smith reasoned that the high mortality rate might have resulted from the inferior pasture conditions in combination with the large amount of snow the park received that winter. He also suggested that the high death rate could be attributed to a cycle in which more of the animals died in some years than in others.[131]

It was clear to others, however, that more than weather conditions or life cycles caused these fatalities. The high number of deaths was somewhat alarming in light of the crisis experienced by the Kaibab Forest Reserve in

Arizona. There, deer had been under protection in a park void of predators. Numbering 3,000 to 4,000 in 1906, the deer, by 1924, had exploded to a population estimated as high as 100,000 animals. Thousands died from starvation.[132] Reflecting on the death of the deer in Buffalo National Park, Hoyes Lloyd, the Parks Branch ornithologist, referred to the report of the Kaibab Investigation Committee and deduced that the crisis in Arizona had much to do with overpopulation. Investigators found "that not only were there too many deer in the territory to subsist on the available food, but that the range was so greatly depleted that it was in imminent danger of being totally destroyed." Lloyd had made the obvious connection to the situation at Buffalo National Park:

> The Park is far too heavily populated with Buffalo, Elk, and Deer for the health of the animals, and if the existing overcrowding be permitted to continue, there is little doubt that Nature will take a decisive hand in reducing the herds in spite of human efforts to keep them in a healthy condition.[133]

There was also concern over how the other animal populations were contributing to the spread of disease among the bison. *Fascioloides magna*, or liver fluke, had also increased in severity among the bison since it was discovered in 1923. The parasite, which seemed to attack elk, caused "malnutrition with a tendency to dropsy and anaemia." In 1923, Hadwen named the parasite as the most serious disease, next to tuberculosis, found at Wainwright.[134] Whereas 5 to 10 per cent of the livers examined were injured by the parasite in the 1922–23 cull, in the 1934–35 slaughter, livers of 28.4 per cent of bison were condemned because they were infested with liver fluke.[135]

From 1932–34, W. E. Swales of the Animal Diseases Research Institute investigated the Visitor's Park, made up of Mott Lake enclosure and Home Paddock, and the Peterson enclosure,[136] and found a species of snail, *Fossaria*, to be the primary host of this parasite. He determined that Mott Lake enclosure was the centre of the infection.[137] The elk and yak in the Visitor's Park and elk in the Peterson enclosure displayed acute symptoms of the disease. This high incidence was likely induced by the crowded conditions of the paddock as autopsies performed on birds and muskrats also showed that they were severely afflicted with the parasite.[138]

When Swales began his investigation, he did not observe symptoms of the parasite in the bison or elk in the main park.[139] However, evidence from the 1934–35 cull proved the parasite had spread to the main bison herd. By 1937–38, Inspector J. S. Bowie found that the parasite was occurring more often in the younger bison.[140] Most interesting was the fact that the bison were not believed to be a secondary host to this liver fluke under normal conditions. Rather, Swales found evidence that the overcrowded conditions heightened the bison's vulnerability to the parasite. He added,

> elk, and possibly to a lesser degree, deer, have offered evidence which would indicate that their susceptibility as secondary hosts of the fluke, constitutes a very real menace to the health of buffalo when both species of animal are permitted to roam and graze at large, the contamination being communicated to the buffalo through faecula of the elk (or deer) being deposited on the grasses and in the waters of lakes and streams.[141]

Investigations of the park continued until its closure and the recommendations echoed the findings of earlier reports. Inspector H. W. Cowan, performed investigations for the Health of Animals Branch, Department of Agriculture in 1936 and 1937. In 1936, the park was experiencing drought conditions. While the bison appeared in healthy condition, he recommended the herd be reduced to 5,000 head, including that year's natural increase, as there was uncertainty about the quantity of feed that would be available. While the animals appeared healthy the following year, the slaughter reports showed tuberculosis was on the increase among the bison and had been steadily rising for a period of years. He believed it necessary to build up a new, disease-free herd.[142]

In 1939, the year the park closed, Dr. Hadwen observed that the winter grazing was good but the summer range was in very poor condition from drought and overgrazing, being covered with inedible weeds, mainly sage. He found tuberculosis ravaging the herd and believed there was no way to eliminate disease without eradicating the whole herd.[143] He wrote, "Personally I feel that in view of the existence of tuberculosis alone in the park that all the large animals should be killed. I made a strong plea for this in 1923 and I feel the same now."[144]

By performing the roles of both zookeepers and breeders, the Parks Branch paralleled the policy that had been initiated by Howard Douglas in the early mountain parks. While the display paddock did attract tourists, this prairie park was never able to fulfill its role as a breeding ground successfully. The park's closed borders meant that the game populations could not expand outside the park and it was never the intention of the park to release the bison. Instead, they contributed to the park's overcrowded conditions. Even with attempts to downsize the bison herd through annual culls, the animals in the park continued to exceed the carrying capacity, and the range was never permitted to recover.

While several investigations were carried out from the early 1920s to the park's closure, the Parks Branch found their hands tied when it came implementing any significant remedies. Clearly, the enthusiasm that the Dominion government had shown for the bison saving effort had waned shortly after the park was established. Problems escalated with the growth of the herd and the Parks Branch was not given enough money to ensure Buffalo National Park functioned properly. By the 1930s, with the onset of the Great Depression, funding to make improvements at the park was not the government's priority. The cost of maintaining an overpopulated animal herd continued to tax the effort until the park's closure and the controversy over reducing the populations of game species only added to this problem. The overpopulation problem only served to exacerbate the spread of tuberculosis through the herd. The Parks Branch was never successful in eliminating or even reducing tuberculosis in the bison herd, and this was one of the main reasons for the park's closure.

1. LAC, J. B. Harkin to Hoyes Lloyd, 6 Mar. 1933, Parks Branch Files, Buffalo National Park [BNP], RG 84, Vol. 50, File BU217, pt. 1.

2. The department sought advice from the Chief Game Guardian for Alberta and the Alberta Fish and Game Association over the issue of reducing the deer, moose, and elk that were in the park, one of the main indications that these animals were considered game and treated differently from the bison. See LAC, Parks Canada Files, BNP, RG 84, Vol. 50, File BU217, pt. 1.

3. Marty, *A Grand and Fabulous Notion*, 82–83.

4. Foster, *Working for Wildlife*, 56.

5. Marty, *A Grand and Fabulous Notion*, 82–83.

6. Marty, *A Grand and Fabulous Notion*, 83–84.

7. Foster, *Working for Wildlife*, 56.

8. Foster, *Working for Wildlife*, 72, 74.

9. LAC, L. Pereira to Howard Douglas, 17 Dec. 1910, Parks Canada Files, BNP, RG 84, Vol. 55, File BU234, pt. 1; LAC, Extract from Letter from Howard Douglas, 26 Sept. 1910, Parks Canada Files, BNP, RG 84, Vol. 50, File BU211, pt. 1.

10. LAC, Maxwell Graham to J. B. Harkin, 4 Dec. 1915, Parks Canada Files, BNP, RG 84, Vol. 55, File BU234, pt. 1.

11. LAC, J. B. Harkin to R. M. Anderson, 23 Jun. 1933, Parks Canada Files, BNP, RG 84, Vol. 50, File BU211, pt. 2.

12. E. J. Cotton, *Buffalo Bud: Adventures of a Cowboy* (Vancouver 1981), 109.

13. Canyon Antelope Reserve, which became Wawaskesy Park, and Menissawok Park, near Maple Creek, Saskatchewan, were set aside in 1914. Nemiskam Park, near Nemiskam, Alberta was established in 1915. These became national parks in 1922. Lothian, *A History of Canada's National Parks*, 42–45.

14. LAC, Extract from Letter from Howard Douglas, 26 Sept. 1910, Parks Canada Files, BNP, RG 84, Vol. 50, File BU211, pt. 1.

15. LAC, Extract from Letter from Howard Douglas, 26 Sep. 1910, Parks Canada Files, BNP, RG 84, Vol. 50, File BU211, pt. 1.

16. Scribner, *Transitions*, 28.

17. "Buffalo Park," map, [circa 1912]. On a 1924 map, the area is labelled "The Home Paddock for buffalo and elk." LAC, "Buffalo Park," map, 1924, Parks Canada Files, BNP, RG 84, Vol. 50, File BU38, pt. 1.

18. LAC, A. G. Smith to Ernest T. Seton, 28 Dec. 1925, Parks Canada Files, BNP, RG 84, Vol. 55, File BU241, pt. 1.

19. *Home of the Buffalo*, VHS, with commentary by Ray Sharp (n.d.), Battle River Historical Society Archives, Wainwright, AB.

20. *Wainwright Star*, 15 May 1918, "Report Shows Buffalo Increase."

21. *Edmonton Bulletin*, 26 Apr. 1930, "Wainwright: Home of the Large Buffalo Herd in Captivity."

22. BNPFA, Diary of Davey Davison, Jan. 1 – Dec. 31, 1929, Davison fonds.

23. LAC, Superintendent of Rocky Mountains Park to the Secretary of the Department of the Interior, 9 Sept. 1910, Parks Canada Files, BNP, RG 84, Vol. 50, File BU211, pt. 1.

24. LAC, A. B. Macdonald to Secretary, Department of the Interior, 27 Apr. 1911, Parks Canada Files, BNP, RG 84, Vol. 50, File BU211, pt. 1.

25. LAC, Maxwell Graham to Mr. Harkin, 3 Aug. 1912, Parks Canada Files, BNP, RG 84, Vol. 53, File BU232, pt. 1.

26. LAC, F. H. Byshe to Mr. Campbell, 24 Mar. 1911, Parks Canada Files, BNP, RG 84, Vol. 50, File BU211, pt. 1.

27. LAC, Edgar McHugh to J. B. Harkin, 31 Jan. 1929, Parks Canada Files, BNP, RG 84, Vol. 50, File BU211, pt. 1.

28. LAC, Edgar McHugh to J. B. Harkin, 31 Jan. 1929, Parks Canada Files, BNP, RG 84, Vol. 50, File BU211, pt. 1.

29. LAC, S. E. Clarke to Commissioner, 1 Aug. 1929, Parks Canada Files, BNP, RG 84, Vol. 50, File BU211, pt. 1.

30. Cotton, *Buffalo Bud*, 110.

31. Hewitt, *Conservation of the Wild Life of Canada*, 238.

32. LAC, S. E. Clarke, "Report on Investigation of Pasture Conditions at Buffalo National Park," Sept. 1930, Parks Canada Files, BNP, RG 84, Vol. 50, File BU35, pt. 1.

33. LAC, Commissioner to Superintendent, 5 Nov. 1917, Parks Canada Files, BNP, RG 84, Vol. 55, File BU262, pt. 1; LAC, A. G. Smith to Chief Superintendent, Dominion Parks, 10 Nov. 1916 and Commissioner to P. C. Bernard Hervey, 21 Nov. 1916, Parks Canada Files, BNP, RG 84, Vol. 55, File BU234, pt. 1.

34. LAC, W. E. D. McTaggart to P.C. Barnard Hervey, 18 Sep. 1913, Parks Canada Files, BNP, RG 84, Vol. 55, File BU262, pt. 1.

35. Coyotes were also called prairie wolves. Hewitt, *Conservation of the Wild Life of Canada*, 194.

36. LAC, Annie S. Armstrong to William J. Roche, 22 Sep. 1917, Parks Canada Files, BNP, RG 84, Vol. 55, File BU262, pt. 1.

37. LAC, P.C. Barnard Hervey to J. B. Harkin, 13 Dec. 1916, Parks Canada Files, BNP, RG 84, Vol. 55, File BU262, pt. 1.

38. LAC, A. G. Smith to Commissioner, 26 Dec. 1917 and Maxwell Graham to Commissioner, 13 May 1918, Parks Canada Files, BNP, RG 84, Vol. 55, File BU262, pt. 1.

39. LAC, A. G. Smith to Commissioner, 26 Dec. 1917, Parks Canada Files, BNP, RG 84, Vol. 55, File BU262, pt. 1.

40. LAC, A. G. Smith to Commissioner, 21 Nov. 1918, Commissioner to Superintendent, 26 Nov. 1918, and P. C. Bernard Hervey to J. B. Harkin, 13 Dec. 1916, Parks Canada Files, BNP, RG 84, Vol. 55, File BU262, pt. 1.

41. LAC, J. B. Harkin to Superintendent, 8 Oct. 1928, Parks Canada Files, BNP, RG 84, Vol. 55, File BU262, pt. 1.

42. LAC, A. G. Smith to Commissioner, 24 Dec. 1934, Parks Canada Files, BNP, RG 84, Vol. 55, File BU262, pt. 1.

43. LAC, A. G. Smith to Commissioner, 21 Jan. 1935, Parks Canada Files, BNP, RG 84, Vol. 55, File BU262, pt. 1. In 1935, J. B. Harkin outlined the new predator policy: "the presence of coyotes is highly desirable as a control measure for deer, gophers, rabbits, etc., all of which destroy pasture, and that the coyotes play a particularly important part in keeping rabbits under control and in so doing are directly beneficial to the grazing animals." LAC, J. B. Harkin to Superintendent, 8 Jan. 1935, Parks Canada Files, BNP, RG 84, Vol. 55, File BU262, pt. 1.

44. The elk depopulation was the first and only organized game cull in the park. The meat was shipped to the Indian Affairs branches in Manitoba and Saskatchewan to be used for Native relief. LAC, *Edmonton Journal*, 24 Nov. 1938, "Slaughter of 1,200 Bisons Starts in Wainwright Park," Parks Canada Files, BNP, RG 84, Vol. 58, File BU299, pt. 14.

45. LAC, George M. Spargo to A. G. Smith, 7 Dec. 1932, Parks Canada Files, BNP, RG 84, Vol. 50, File BU211, pt. 2.

46. LAC, George M. Spargo to A. G. Smith, 7 Dec. 1932, Parks Canada Files, BNP, RG 84, Vol. 50, File BU211, pt. 2.

47. LAC, Extract from a report by Dr. Hadwen, 21 Feb. 1923, quoted in Memorandum to J. B. Harkin, 15 Feb. 1933, Parks Canada Files, BNP, RG 84, Vol. 50, File BU217, pt. 1.

48. LAC, Commissioner to Superintendent, 13 Apr. 1923, Parks Canada Files, BNP, RG 84, Vol. 50, File BU217, pt. 1.

49. LAC, Benjamin Lawton to J. B. Harkin, 16 May 1923, Parks Canada Files, BNP, RG 84, Vol. 50, File BU217, pt. 1.

50. LAC, Report by S. H. Clark, 14 Oct. 1932, Parks Canada Files, BNP, RG 84, Vol. 50, File BU211, pt. 2.

51. For example, Buffalo National Park shipped a carload of elk to Ontario for their Game Department in November 1932. LAC, A. G. Smith to Geo. M. Spargo, 23 Jan. 1933, Parks Canada Files, BNP, RG 84, Vol. 55, File BU234, pt. 1.

52. LAC, A. E. Etter to J. B. Harkin, 19 Jun. 1933 and 30 Sept. 1933, A. Bryan Williams to J. B. Harkin, 20 Jun. 1933, 27 Jun. 1933 and 31 Aug. 1931, Parks Canada Files, BNP, RG 84, Vol. 55, File BU234, pt. 1.

53. LAC, Benjamin Lawton to J. B. Harkin, 3 Oct. 1923, Parks Canada Files, BNP, RG 84, Vol. 50, File BU217, pt. 1.

54. LAC, J. B. Harkin to A. Bryan Williams, 6 Jun. 1933, Parks Canada Files, BNP, RG 84, Vol. 55, File BU234, pt. 1.

55. LAC, J. B. Harkin to H. H. Rowatt, 7 Dec. 1933, Parks Canada Files, BNP, RG 84, Vol. 50, File BU211, pt. 2.

56. LAC, George M. Spargo to A. G. Smith, 7 Dec. 1932, Parks Canada Files, BNP, RG 84, Vol. 50, File BU211, pt. 2.

57. LAC, J. B. Harkin to S. H. Clark, 6 Jun. 1933, Parks Canada Files, BNP, RG 84, Vol. 50, File BU211, pt. 2.

58. LAC, Hoyes Lloyd to Mr. Harkin, 15 Sept. 1933, Parks Canada Files, BNP, RG 84, Vol. 50, File BU211, pt. 2.

59. LAC, J. B. Harkin to S. H. Clark, 13 Oct. 1933, Parks Canada Files, BNP, RG 84, Vol. 50, File BU211, pt. 2.

60. LAC, S. H. Clark to J. B. Harkin, 18 Nov. 1933, Parks Canada Files, BNP, RG 84, Vol. 50, File BU211, pt. 2.

61. LAC, Hoyes Lloyd to J. B. Harkin, 11 Sept. 1933, Parks Canada Files, BNP, RG 84, Vol. 50, File BU211, pt. 2.

62. LAC, A. G. Smith to Commissioner, 5 Jun. 1934, and A. G. Smith to Commissioner, 9 Jan. 1935, Parks Canada Files, BNP, RG 84, Vol. 50, File BU211, pt. 2.

63. LAC, A. G. Smith to Commissioner, 10 May 1935, Parks Canada Files, BNP, RG 84, Vol. 50, File BU211, pt. 2.

64. LAC, A. G. Smith to Commissioner, 4 Jun. 1936, Parks Canada Files, BNP, RG 84, Vol. 50, File BU211, pt. 2.

65. LAC, J. B. Harkin to Game Commissioner, 18 Jun. 1936, Parks Canada Files, BNP, RG 84, Vol. 50, File BU211, pt. 2.

66. LAC, Seymour Hadwen to J. B. Harkin, 21 Feb. 1923, Parks Canada Files, BNP, RG 84, Vol. 58, BU299-2, pt. 1.

67. LAC, Seymour Hadwen to J. B. Harkin, 21 Feb. 1923, Parks Canada Files, BNP, RG 84, Vol. 58, BU299-2, pt. 1.

68. LAC, Seymour Hadwen to J. B. Harkin, 21 Feb. 1923, Parks Canada Files, BNP, RG 84, Vol. 58, BU299-2, pt. 1.

69. LAC, Seymour Hadwen to J. B. Harkin, 21 Feb. 1923, Parks Canada Files, BNP, RG 84, Vol. 58, BU299-2, pt. 1.

70. LAC, A. G. Smith, Copy of a statement handed in at the close of operations by Dr. I. Christian, Veterinary Inspector-in-charge, 1923, Parks Canada Files, BNP, RG 84, Vol. 58, BU299-2, pt. 1.

71. LAC, Seymour Hadwen to J. B. Harkin, 21 Feb. 1923, Parks Canada Files, BNP, RG 84, Vol. 58, BU299-2, pt. 1.

72. LAC, Frederick Torrance to J.B. Harkin, 27 Mar. 1923, Parks Canada Files, BNP, RG 84, Vol. 58, File BU299-2, pt. 1.

73. LAC, Maxwell Graham to Mr. Harkin, 3 Aug. 1912 and "Report: The Canadian Government Buffalo Herds for Calendar Year Ending Dec. 31, 1915," Parks Canada Files, BNP, RG 84, Vol. 52, File BU232, pt. 1.

74. University of Alberta Archives, Edmonton, AB (hereafter UAA), T.B. at Buffalo Park between Dec. 1916 to Jan. 1st, 1922, Buffalo National Park Files, 2002-18-4.

75. LAC, The handwritten notes in this memorandum, which indicate that tuberculosis was suspected, appear to belong to Maxwell Graham. A. G. Smith to J. B. Harkin, 8 Jun. 1917, Parks Canada Files, BNP, RG 84, Vol. 53, File BU232, pt. 1.

76. LAC, "Report: The Canadian Government Buffalo Herds for Calendar Year Ending Dec. 31, 1915," Parks Canada Files, BNP, RG 84, Vol. 52, File BU232, pt. 1; LAC, Memorandum to R. A. Gibson, Report of Dr. Seymour Hadwen on Elk and Wainwright Parks, 15 Sept. 1939, Parks Canada Files, BNP, RG 84, Vol. 52, File BU233, pt. 2.

77. LAC, Superintendent to W. W. Cory, 22 Apr. 1907, Parks Canada Files, BNP, RG 84, Vol. 51, File BU209, pt. 4; LAC, A. G. Smith, "Statement of Original Shipments of Buffalo into Buffalo Park, Wainwright," 14 Sept. 1926, Parks Canada Files, BNP, RG 84, Vol. 51, File BU209, pt. 3.

78. LAC, Frederick Torrance to J.B. Harkin, 27 Mar. 1923, Parks Canada Files, BNP, RG 84, Vol. 58, File BU299-2, pt. 1.

79. LAC, Seymour Hadwen to J. B. Harkin, 21 Feb. 1923, Parks Canada Files, BNP, RG 84, Vol. 58, BU299-2, pt. 1.

80. LAC, J. B. Harkin to Mr. Cory, 23 May 1923, Parks Canada Files, BNP, RG 84, Vol. 58, BU299-2, pt. 1.

81. UAA, Memorandum from Maxwell Graham, 19 Mar. 1919, Buffalo National Park Files, 2002-18-4.

82. LAC, Frederick Torrance to J.B. Harkin, 27 Mar. 1923, Parks Canada Files, BNP, RG 84, Vol. 58, File BU299-2, pt. 1.

83. UAA, Maxwell Graham quoted in Maxwell Graham to J. B. Harkin, 7 Jul. 1916, Buffalo National Park Files, 2002-18-4.

84. LAC, Seymour Hadwen to J. B. Harkin, 21 Feb. 1923, Parks Canada Files, BNP, RG 84, Vol. 58, BU299-2, pt. 1.

85. LAC, J. B. Harkin to Mr. Cory, 23 May 1923, Parks Canada Files, BNP, RG 84, Vol. 58, BU299-2, pt. 1.

86. LAC, J. B. Harkin to Mr. Cory, 23 May 1923, Parks Canada Files, BNP, RG 84, Vol. 58, BU299-2, pt. 1.

87. LAC, E. A. Watson to Dr. Geo Hilton, 4 Apr. 1924, Parks Canada Files, BNP, RG 84, Vol. 58, BU299-2, pt. 1.

88. Tuberculosis in the bison herd went unmentioned except for one passing reference that alluded to the disease's possible connection with lung worms. Cameron stated, "The lesions associated with these worms were emphysema and hard areas which suggested tuberculosis when felt from the outside. The numbers found in a single buffalo were comparatively few, about a dozen." LAC, A. E. Cameron, "Notes on Buffalo: Anatomy, Pathological Conditions, and Parasites," reprinted from the *Veterinary Journal* 79 (10), Parks Canada Files, BNP, RG 84, Vol. 58, BU299-2, pt. 1.

89. LAC, E. A. Watson to Dr. Geo Hilton, 4 Apr. 1924 and J. B. Harkin to J. H. Grisdale, 6 May 1924, Parks Canada Files, BNP, RG 84, Vol. 58, BU299-2, pt. 1.

90. A. E. Cameron, "Some Further Notes on Buffalo," *Veterinary Journal* 80 (1924) 417.

91. LAC, Acting Veterinary General to J. B. Harkin, 25 Aug. 1928 and J. B. Harkin to R. G. Ferguson, 4 Sept. 1928, Parks Canada Files, BNP, RG 84, Vol. 58, BU299-2, pt. 1.

92. LAC, Seymour Hadwen to J. B. Harkin, 21 Feb. 1923 and Frederick Torrance to J.B. Harkin, 27 Mar. 1923, Parks Canada Files, BNP, RG 84, Vol. 58, BU299-2, pt. 1.

93. LAC, Memorandum to Mr. Cory, 23 May 1923, Parks Canada Files, BNP, RG 84, Vol. 58, File BU299-2, pt. 1.

94. LAC, Howard Douglas to W. W. Cory, 15 Jun. 1906, Parks Canada Files, BNP, RG 84, Vol. 51, File BU209, pt. 1.

95. LAC, Extract from a report of Dr. Torrance, Veterinary Director General, 27 Mar. 1923, quoted in Memorandum to J. B. Harkin, 15 Feb. 1933, Parks Canada Files, BNP, RG 84, Vol. 50, File BU217, pt. 1.

96. In 1918, a newspaper article reported that 8,000 bushels of oats were threshed at Buffalo National Park, of which 2,100 bushels were shipped to other parks. That same year, 1,200 tons of hay were cut and stacked and permits were given out to settlers covering the cutting of 671 tons of hay. *Edmonton Journal*, 11 Apr. 1918, "537 Increase in Buffalo at Wainwright Park," LAC, Parks Canada Files, BNP, RG 84, Vol. 53, File BU232, pt. 1.

97. LAC, Extract from letter of Superintendent, 26 Mar. 1925, quoted in Memorandum to J. B. Harkin, 15 Feb. 1933, Parks Canada Files, BNP, RG 84, Vol. 50, File BU217, pt. 1.

98. LAC, A. G. Smith to J. B. Harkin, 18 Mar. 1925, Parks Canada Files, BNP, RG 84, Vol. 52, File BU232-1, pt. 1.

99. LAC, A. G. Smith to Commissioner, 14 Oct. 1924, Parks Canada Files, BNP, RG 84, Vol. 52, File BU232-1, pt. 1.

100. LAC, J. B. Harkin to W. W. Cory, 3 Feb. 1925 and A. G. Smith to Commissioner, 10 Feb. 1925, Parks Canada Files, BNP, RG 84, Vol. 52, File BU232-1, pt. 1; LAC, Memorandum to Maxwell Graham, 22 Jan. 1925, Parks Canada Files, BNP, RG 84, Vol. 52, File BU232-1, pt. 1.

101. LAC, A. G. Smith to Commissioner, 10 Feb. 1925, Parks Canada Files, BNP, RG 84, Vol. 52, File BU232-1, pt. 1.

102. LAC, A. G. Smith to Commissioner, 10 Feb. 1925, Parks Canada Files, BNP, RG 84, Vol. 52, File BU232-1, pt. 1.

103. LAC, J. B. Harkin to W. W. Cory, 3 Feb. 1925 and Extract from the Superintendent of Buffalo Park, 16 Feb. 1925, Parks Canada Files, BNP, RG 84, Vol. 52, File BU232-1, pt. 1.

104. LAC, A. G. Smith to J. B. Harkin, 18 Mar. 1925, Parks Canada Files, BNP, RG 84, Vol. 52, File BU232-1, pt. 1.

105. LAC, Quoted in Memorandum to W. W. Cory, 15 Jul. 1925, Parks Canada Files, BNP, RG 84, Vol. 52, BU232-1, pt. 2.

106. LAC, Extracts from diary of E. J. Cotton, 13 Aug. 1925 and 15 Aug. 1925, quoted in Memorandum to J. B. Harkin, 15 Feb. 1933, Parks Canada Files, BNP, RG 84, Vol. 50, File BU217, pt. 1.

107. LAC, Extract from letter from Superintendent Smith, 11 Nov. 1926, quoted in Memorandum to J. B. Harkin, 15 Feb. 1933, Parks Canada Files, BNP, RG 84, Vol. 50, File BU217, pt. 1.

108. LAC, C. Nagle to Hoyes Lloyd, 7 May 1927, Parks Canada Files, BNP, RG 84, Vol. 54, File BU232, pt. 4.

109. LAC, "Loss of Buffalo, Buffalo Park," Winter 1926–27 and A. G. Smith to Commissioner, 12 May 1927, Parks Canada Files, BNP, RG 84, Vol. 54, File BU232, pt. 4.

110. LAC, A. G. Smith, Report of 20 Apr. 1927, quoted in C. E. Nagle to Mr. Lloyd, 7 May 1927, Parks Canada Files, BNP, RG 84, Vol. 54, File BU232, pt. 4.

111. Only two of Warden Davey Davison's diaries, the years 1927 and 1929, still exist. A comparison of the two diaries shows that the number of animals that died in 1927 in the Visitor's Park, especially during the winter months, was significantly higher than in 1929. BNPFA, Diary of Davey Davison, Jan. 1, 1927 to Jan. 2, 1928 and Diary of Davey Davison, Jan. 1 – Dec. 31, 1929, Davison fonds.

112. LAC, Extract from letter from Superintendent, 25 Aug. 1927, quoted in Memorandum to J. B. Harkin, 15 Feb. 1933, Parks Canada Files, BNP, RG 84, Vol. 50, File BU217, pt. 1.

113. LAC, Extracts from the diary of E. J. Cotton, Buffalo Park, 25 Apr. 1927, Parks Canada Files, BNP, RG 84, Vol. 52, File BU232-1, pt. 2.

114. LAC, D. H. Christie to O. S. Finnie, 23 Jun. 1927, Parks Canada Files, BNP, RG 84, Vol. 52, File BU232-1, pt. 2.

115. LAC, S. E. Clarke, "Report on Investigation of Pasture Conditions at Buffalo Park," Sept. 1929, Parks Canada Files, BNP, RG 84, Vol. 50, BU35, pt. 1.

116. LAC, S. E. Clarke, Report on Investigation of Pasture Conditions at Buffalo Park," Sept. 1929, Parks Canada Files, BNP, RG 84, Vol. 50, File BU35, pt. 1.

117. LAC, S. E. Clarke, "Report on Investigation of Pasture Conditions at Buffalo Park," Sept. 1929, Parks Canada Files, BNP, RG 84, Vol. 50, BU35, pt. 1.

118. LAC, S. E. Clarke, "Report on Investigation of Pasture Conditions at Buffalo Park," Sept. 1929, Parks Canada Files, BNP, RG 84, Vol. 50, File BU35, pt. 1.

119. LAC, Memorandum to Mr. Spero, 4 Mar. 1931, Parks Canada Files, BNP, RG 84, Vol. 50, File BU217, pt. 1; LAC, S. E. Clarke, "Report on Investigation of Pasture Conditions at Buffalo Park," Sept. 1929 and S. E. Clarke, "Report on Investigation of Pasture Conditions at Buffalo National Park," Sept. 1930, Parks Canada Files, BNP, RG 84, Vol. 50, File BU35, pt. 1.

120. LAC, S. E. Clarke, "Report on Investigation of Pasture Conditions at Buffalo Park," Sept. 1930, Parks Canada Files, BNP, RG 84, Vol. 50, BU35, pt. 1.

121. LAC, S. E. Clarke, "Report on Investigation of Pasture Conditions at Buffalo Park," Sept. 1930, Parks Canada Files, BNP, RG 84, Vol. 50, BU35, pt. 1.

122. LAC, S. E. Clarke, "Report on Investigation of Pasture Conditions at Buffalo Park," Sept. 1930, Parks Canada Files, BNP, RG 84, Vol. 50, BU35, pt. 1.

123. LAC, S. E. Clarke, "Report on Investigation of Pasture Conditions at Buffalo Park," Sept. 1929, Parks Canada Files, BNP, RG 84, Vol. 50, BU35, pt. 1.

124. LAC, Hoyes Lloyd to J. B. Harkin, 15 Feb. 1933, Parks Canada Files, BNP, RG 84, Vol. 57, File BU299, pt. 9.

125. LAC, Extract from letter of Superintendent, 24 Feb. 1932, quoted in Memorandum to J. B. Harkin, 15 Feb. 1933, Parks Canada Files, BNP, RG 84, Vol. 50, File BU217, pt. 1.

126. LAC, Extract from Diary of Warden Cotton, 20 May 1932, quoted in Memorandum to J. B. Harkin, 15 Feb. 1933, Parks Canada Files, BNP, RG 84, Vol. 50, File BU217, pt. 1.

127. LAC, Memorandum to J. B. Harkin, 15 Feb. 1933, Parks Canada Files, BNP, RG 84, Vol. 50, BU217, pt. 1.

128. LAC, A. G. Smith to Commissioner, 20 Mar. 1931, Parks Canada Files, BNP, RG 84, Vol. 50, File BU217, pt. 1.

129. LAC, Quoted in Letter to Mr. Williamson, 14 Aug. 1937, Parks Canada Files, BNP, RG 84, Vol. 55, File BU234, pt. 1.

130. LAC, A. G. Smith to Commissioner, 10 Feb. 1932, Parks Canada Files, BNP, RG 84, Vol. 50, File BU217, pt. 1; LAC, A. G. Smith to Commissioner, 6 Jun. 1932, Parks Canada Files, BNP, RG 84, Vol. 52, File BU233, pt. 2.

131. LAC, A. G. Smith to Commissioner, 10 Feb. 1932, Parks Canada Files, BNP, RG 84, Vol. 50, File BU217, pt. 1.

132. John P. Russo, *The Kaibab North Deer Herd: Its History, Problems and Management* (Phoenix 1964), 37, 45–46.

133. LAC, Hoyes Lloyd to J. B. Harkin, 22 Aug. 1932, Parks Canada Files, BNP, RG 84, Vol. 50, File BU217, pt. 1.

134. LAC, Seymour Hadwen to J. B. Harkin, 21 Feb. 1923, Parks Canada Files, BNP, RG 84, Vol. 58, File BU299-2, pt. 1.

135. LAC, A. G. Smith to W. E. Swales, 18 Feb. 1935, Parks Canada Files, BNP, RG 84, Vol. 52, File BU233, pt. 2.

136. LAC, Thomas W. M. Cameron to J. B. Harkin, 21 Jul. 1933, Parks Canada Files, BNP, RG 84, Vol. 52, File BU233, pt. 2. The Peterson enclosure was located on the eastern border, in the northeast section of the park just south of the Visitor's Park. LAC, "Buffalo Park," map, 1926, Parks Canada Files, BNP, RG 84, Vol. 50, File BU38, pt. 1.

137. LAC, Attachment to memorandum, Hoyes Lloyd to Mr. Powell, 11 May 1935, and Thomas W. M. Cameron to J. B. Harkin, 21 Jul. 1933, Parks Canada Files, BNP, RG 84, Vol. 52, File BU233, pt. 2.

138. LAC, A Summarized Report of the Investigation of Parasitism in the Animals at Buffalo Park, Wainwright, Alta., with Special Reference to the Life History and Control of the Large Liver Fluke (*Fasciola magna*), n.d., Parks Canada Files, BNP, RG 84, Vol. 52, File BU233, pt. 2.

139. LAC, A Summarized Report, Parks Canada Files, BNP, RG 84, Vol. 52, File BU233, pt. 2.

140. LAC, A. G. Smith to W. E. Swales, 18 Feb. 1935 and J. S. Bowie to Veterinary Director General, 20 Jan. 1938, Parks Canada Files, BNP, RG 84, Vol. 52, File BU233, pt. 2.

141. LAC, Attachment to memorandum, Hoyes Lloyd to Mr. Powell, 11 May 1935, Parks Canada Files, BNP, RG 84, Vol. 52, File BU233, pt. 2.

142. LAC, H. W. Cowan, Report of Inspector, 23 Jul. 1936 and H. W. Cowan, Report of Inspector, 12 Mar. 1937, Parks Canada Files, BNP, RG 84, Vol. 52, File BU233, pt. 2.

143. LAC, Memorandum to R. A. Gibson, Report of Dr. Seymour Hadwen on Elk and Wainwright Parks, 15 Sept. 1939, Parks Canada Files, BNP, RG 84, Vol. 52, File BU233, pt, 2.

144. LAC, Seymour Hadwen to F. H. H. Williamson, 7 Dec. 1939, Parks Canada Files, BNP, RG 84, Vol. 982, File BU2[548608], pt. 3.

CHAPTER FIVE

"Evolving the Arctic Cow"

Crossbreeding, Disease, and the Demise of
Buffalo National Park, 1926–1939

IN 1916, THE PARKS BRANCH AND DEPARTMENT OF AGRICULTURE initiated a crossbreeding experiment inside the borders of Buffalo National Park. The purpose of this project was to cross the plains bison with domestic cattle in hopes of creating a new breed—the cattalo[1]—that would be more adaptable to the cold Canadian climate and at the same time exhibit a better quality and quantity of beef. The cattalo experiment was unique in the Canadian national parks. It was introduced to the park during an era when hybrid experimentation was taking place in Canada and elsewhere, as early 20th century science tried to improve plants and animals for human use.[2]

As the Dominion government and the Parks Branch considered these hybridization trials a separate initiative from the bison effort, the cattalo experiment was a deliberate attempt to make the bison at Wainwright useful. This experiment, however, introduced a number of problems and contradictions for the park. The decision to move the experiment to Buffalo National Park not only jeopardized the bison effort in principle, but also posed a threat to the health of the bison herd. The issue of hybridization and concern over the spread of disease resurfaced with the transfer of plains bison north. The government's response to protests, however, shows that while they were aware of the gravity of the issues, this was secondary to finding a quick fix to the problems at the Wainwright bison effort. We are still realizing the consequences of this decision today.

Bison–domestic cattle hybrids were by no means new to the 20th century. The earliest account of this hybrid cross was recorded by Peter Kalm in 1750; he stated that calves of wild cows and oxen were found in Carolina and in provinces south of Pennsylvania. By 1800, such hybrids were said to be common in the northern counties of Virginia.[3] Much of the early hybridization between bison and cattle resulted from raising captured bison calves with domestic cattle herds.[4] In fact, the first hybrid on Michel Pablo and Charles

Allard's ranch occurred because they ranged a bison bull and domestic cow together. Friends of Pablo recalled that he was "enthused over the new creature, and envisioned a profitable future for its kind. Other cattlemen were of like opinion, and carefully planned efforts to raise cattalo were made."[5] Eventually the Pablo-Allard cattalo herd numbered from 150 to 200 head.[6]

While most early hybrids occurred naturally when captured bison calves were raised with domestic cattle, soon more systematic attempts were undertaken to create a new breed. Beginning his trials in 1815 and continuing for almost thirty years, Robert Wickliffe of Lexington, Kentucky, was one of the first to begin seriously experimenting with hybridizing bison.[7] In the 1890s, C. "Buffalo" Jones of Kansas and Charles Goodnight of Texas became famous and influential in their efforts in crossbreeding bison.[8] Jones lost two-thirds of his domestic calves in a severe blizzard during the winter of 1885–86: "I determined to engraft this blood of a hardy race upon our domestic cattle, and secure, if possible, all the hardiness and good sense of the buffalo and the mild disposition of our native cattle."[9] He devoted the next 20 years to producing a cattalo breed. While his experiments were very costly and suffered many obstacles, Jones successfully bred bison bulls to Galloway, Polled Angus, and range cows.[10] In 1906 he boasted, "Our cattalo company now [has] sixty head of magnificent animals; many of the cows weigh over a ton, and their meat is far more desirable than the choicest beef, while their robes are so much more valuable than the robes of the buffalo, that they cannot be mentioned in the same breath."[11]

Like Jones, Charles Goodnight also crossed Polled Angus cattle with bison in hopes of developing a new breed.[12] He believed that the infusion of bison blood gave his hybrids several advantages over ordinary range cattle. Cattalo were hardy and able to withstand blizzards. They also had a better survival rate when in a weakened condition because cattalo, like bison, used their forelegs rather than hind feet to rise. Goodnight also believed cattalo to be immune from the diseases that afflicted cattle herds, such as Texas blackleg and Texan fever. In terms of their beef qualities, they consumed less, but put on greater weight than domestic breeds, even under adverse conditions. He reported that his cattalo cut 150 pounds more than the domestic herds, and the meat was of better quality than beef. [13]

While Buffalo Jones boasted that he was the first person to have conducted successful experiments to cross bison with domestic cattle,[14] it appears that, in fact, Colonel Samuel Bedson of Manitoba began his experiments earlier than Jones. In 1880, Bedson, warden at the Stoney Mountain

Penitentiary near Winnipeg, Manitoba, bought eight bison,[15] some of the progeny of the herd that James McKay captured in 1873, with a $1,000 loan from Donald Smith, Chief Commissioner of the Hudson's Bay Company. He pastured these bison on the prison grounds and later began crossbreeding them with Durham cattle.[16] In 1886, the year Jones claimed to have begun his experiments, naturalist Ernest Thompson Seton, in "A List of the Mammals of Manitoba," praised Bedson's hybrid crosses:

> The hybrid animal is [claimed] to be a great improvement on both of its progenitors, as it is more docile and a better milker than the Buffalo, but retains its hardihood, whilst the robe is finer, darker and more even, and the general shape of the animal is improved by the reduction of the hump and increased proportion of the hind-quarters.[17]

George Colpitts argues that Bedson's motive behind raising bison and experimenting with hybridization resulted from the food scarcities that began to surface in the West in the 1870s. Bedson believed that the bison–domestic cattle cross was one of the only solutions to solving the food supply problem, which had been exacerbated by the near extermination of the bison. By the 1890s, Colpitts argues, interest in domestication and hybridization waned because of the increase in field crops and animal husbandry, the availability of scientific advice, and the land booms that followed the election of a Liberal administration in 1896.[18] While Colpitts suggests that interest in hybridization ceased because it was no longer needed to maintain stability and social structures in Manitoba, in fact, there was still widespread interest in hybridization in Canada. From the time the Dominion government first acquired bison for Rocky Mountains Park in 1897, the authority administrating the national parks, later the Parks Branch, received requests from private individuals to purchase bison for crossbreeding purposes.[19] By 1900, the Dominion government itself became linked to hybridization experiments when Rocky Mountains Park loaned Mossom Boyd, a man from Bobcaygeon, Ontario, an aged bison bull, for use in his private experiments.[20]

Boyd's cattalo experiment is significant because it was taken over by the Dominion government in 1915 and the herd was moved to Buffalo National Park. Boyd began his hybridization experiment in 1894 when he crossed a purebred bison bull, which he had obtained the previous year from B. C. Winston of Monterey, California, with several different breeds of domestic cows.[21] The purpose behind his crossbreeding experiments was the same as previous experimenters—to produce a hardier breed of range cattle that would

The cattalo herd at Buffalo National Park. Photo by J. H. Gano.

withstand "the severe climate of our Western Provinces, and also to combine the large carcass and the fine robe of the buffalo with the better beef qualities of the domestic breeds."[22] Of all the experiments up to this point, Boyd's three-stage process appears to have been the most methodological. The first stage involved crossing bison with domestic cattle. The second stage was to cross the hybrid product from the first stage with a purebred animal of either bison or domestic cattle descent. The final stage, the phase Boyd's experiment had reached by 1913, involved breeding two animals, both of mixed blood, with each other. Boyd identified the progeny from each stage by a different title. The animal resulting from the first cross was called hybrid buffalo or just a hybrid. In the second stage, the offspring was identified by the percentage of bison blood in the cross (i.e., ¾ buffalo). Boyd called only the animals produced in the third stage, where both parents were of mixed blood, cattalo.[23]

Initially, Howard Douglas' interest in hybridization was one of curiosity. In 1903, the superintendent of Rocky Mountains Park sent another bison bull to Boyd for his experiment in exchange for two hybrid bison cows crossed with polled Angus and Gallaway.[24] Douglas, agreed to Boyd's request because he thought the addition of the hybrids would make Rocky Mountains Park unique:

> Since the Park is [k]eeping animals for the public interest and amuse-ment these animals might as well be made to serve a further useful purpose[.]
>
> This would be something in line with the work done by Government experimental farms and would distinguish the Banff Park from those in the United [States] in [which] every principal city has a small herd of pure Buffaloes.[25]

However, the Dominion government's interest in these experiments soon moved beyond mere amusement. In 1911, the two hybrid heifers were disposed of because F. H. Byshe, of the Department of the Interior, thought the government's focus should be on developing purebred animals and that the hybrids "detracted from the impression made upon visitors by the pure breds."[26] However, the slaughter of these two hybrids probably created even more interest in this field of experimentation because of the quality of the meat. Mr. Colebrook, the butcher, was favourably impressed as he had never seen beef so fat.[27] In a letter to Parks Branch Commissioner J. B. Harkin, Douglas concluded:

> This would go to prove that a cross of this nature would be very beneficial for beef purposes...It would seem to justify a further carrying out of an experiment of this kind...So that taking everything into consideration each one of these animals would realize at least double the price of an ordinary domestic cow.[28]

This discovery at Banff appears to have piqued the interest of the Parks Branch. In 1912, Harkin thought his department should offer to give a number of young bison to the Department of Agriculture if they were willing to carry out hybrid experiments. He believed these experiments would produce a greater quality beef animal and "might prove very valuable to the country." He continued, "When there is a possibility of such a result it seems to me that this Department will sooner or later be subject to criticism if it takes no steps on these lines but simply maintains the buffalo for show purposes."[29] By 1918, when the experiment was already in full swing, a copy of a letter, likely penned by Harkin, confirmed the Park Branch's purpose behind the experiment: "While the buffalo has a very distinct value as it stands...various schemes for making the herd of additional value to the people of the west are under consideration. In the first place experiments in cross-breeding are now being carried on at Buffalo Park for this department by the Department of Agriculture."[30]

The cattalo experiment was not only a means to make the bison herd useful, but also an excuse for the Parks Branch to refuse to supply bison to private individuals for their own experiments. The Department of Agriculture had the necessary facilities, equipment, and staff, and if the government undertook its own experiments, Harkin believed this would satisfy the public. Up to this point, neither the United States and Canadian government nor scientific institutions in either country had attempted any crossbreeding experiments, but there had been attempts by private parties in Canada and the United States. While some of the results had been encouraging, some difficulties had been encountered, specifically the deaths of domestic stock used in the experiments. Harkin believed private individuals should not be allowed to conduct experiments because they would not possess the necessary technical information and their failure could taint the government's experiments.[31] Unlike the United States government, the Parks Branch had the ability to limit private experimentation in Canada because the Dominion government had a monopoly on bison.[32]

Like the Parks Branch, the Department of Agriculture was interested in pursuing the experiment. Officials in that department believed that such trials

"King," one of the most famous animals produced by the cattalo experiment, was one of the few hybrids from a bison bull and domestic cow cross. Because of the high incidence of mortality among the cows, this cross was discontinued in favour of the domestic bull and bison cow cross. Photo by J. H. Gano.

had great value for the future of the cattle industry and would put their depart-ment on the cutting edge of scientific advances in hybridization. E. S. Archibald, who became Director of Experimental Farms in 1919 when J. H. Grisdale moved into the position of Deputy Minister of Agriculture, affirmed:

> There is no doubt that the quality of beef and the quantity of high quality beef from these cross-breds is exceptionally good, that the hides will eventually be quite valuable, and that the hardiness of all cattle containing a small percentage of buffalo blood would be in-creased. Aside from this, this line of hybridizing is one which will give excellent correlative figures for all classes of domesticated animals. At the present time no new work in breeding of an experimental nature is being anywhere undertaken, and this would seem a very desirable field; one which would give valuable data of a scientific character.[33]

In 1914, Maxwell Graham, chief of park animals, suggested that perhaps Mossom Boyd's services could be procured to help begin the crossbreeding experiment. That summer, however, Boyd passed away. Since his family was unable to continue his cattalo experiment, Boyd's son G. Cust Boyd, execu-tor of his father's will, approached Martin Burrell, the Minister of Agricul-ture, to see if the government would be interested in taking over his father's experiment.[34] Both the Parks Branch and the Department of Agriculture were interested. The advantage of acquiring Boyd's cattalo was that they could avoid the great expense involved in starting an experiment. Further-more, by purchasing this experiment, they believed that many of the initial difficulties that Boyd and other experimenters had encountered—the high mortality during calving and the problem of sterility—would have already been overcome. Thus, in December 1915, the Department of Agriculture purchased twenty head, sixteen females and four males of mixed blood, from the estate of Mossom Boyd. These animals were shipped from Ontario to the Experimental Farm in Scott, Saskatchewan, where the herd was held until land was made available at Buffalo National Park.[35]

This joint venture was to be overseen and funded by the Department of Agriculture, but J. B. Harkin offered the full co-operation of the Parks Branch. He not only guaranteed that land at Buffalo National Park would be turned over to the experiment, but also promised the Department of Agriculture, upon application, any bison needed for hybridizing or crossbreeding purpos-es.[36] The suggestion that the experimental farm be set up at Buffalo National Park seems to have first come from J. H. Grisdale, Director of the Agriculture

Yak were transferred to Buffalo National Park from Rocky Mountains Park in 1919. Yak, believed to be an intermediate species between bison and domestic cattle, were introduced into the hybrid experiment in hopes that it would help counteract the problem of sterility of the male offspring. Photo by William Carsell.

Experimental Farms.[37] It was the most practical, cost-effective, and feasible solution for the Department of Agriculture. At Wainwright, there was an endless supply of bison, and, as E. S. Archibald noted, "If Crown land could be used for this experiment the cost of a number of years' work would be comparatively light and the results would be worth many times the expenditure."[38] Another reason for situating the experiment at the park was because Grisdale feared that "introducing such experimental work" on one of the Dominion's experimental farms might "discredit [them] in the eyes of the public."[39]

The Parks Branch never considered its involvement in the trials as a conflict of interest. They believed the cattalo experiment was a separate operation from preserving the bison. Although both were operating in the same area, and the bison-saving effort was supplying the cattalo experiment with breeding stock, the experiment was to be operated and managed by the Department of Agriculture. Thus for the Parks Branch the set-up was an ideal way to make use of the herd while not jeopardizing its future.

Soon after their arrival at Wainwright, Boyd's cattalo were exhibiting characteristics that were seen as proof of the animals' worth and the value of the experiment. In 1920, A. G. Smith stated that they were in first-class condition after the winter despite having never been fed.[40] In a letter to Archibald he wrote, "There were times coming on toward spring when the crust would get bad that I thought we would have to begin feeding them, but they came through without getting one pound of feed other than what they rustled, and I will venture to say very few animals in the West did that this year."[41]

While Boyd's cattalo were showing promise, a number of problems with the management of the experiment surfaced almost immediately, which resulted from the two departments sharing the effort. The Parks Branch was responsible for preparing an enclosure before the animals arrived, and then took charge of feeding and caring for them. The cost of running the experiment and the breeding decisions were the responsibility of the Department of Agriculture. In practice, however, the Parks Branch wielded much more power, partly due to the lack of communication between the two departments. Other than herdsman James Wilson, who was hired to look after the cattalo, the Department of Agriculture had no other on-site staff. The others involved in the experiment were park employees: A. G. Smith was paid a salary to oversee the experiment at the park level and the park riders from time to time were called on to help with operations.[42] As a result, much of the decision making was left with A.G. Smith. In 1918, Smith wrote Harkin: "This experiment if it is to be carried out properly requires something more than feeding the animals, and I did not understand from you that I was to continue on in charge of these animals after they were transferred. I have given Mr. Grisdale every assistance I could up to the present, but I wish to know what action I am to take in future."[43]

It should not be surprising that Smith's influence went beyond mere animal care. In fact, in 1920 Smith outlined that year's breeding program. When in March he had not heard yet from Archibald about how the breeding program should proceed that year, he wrote and offered his opinion about how the present animals should be distributed and suggested that two young bison, a male and female, and a heifer bison calf should be added to the experiment. From the correspondence between Archibald and Harkin and A. G. Smith and Archibald, it appears that Smith's recommendations for the breeding plan had been followed to the letter.[44] Maxwell Graham, Chief of the Parks Branch Animal Division, was not impressed with the state of operations at the park. Even prior to 1920, he informed Harkin that Smith, by offering his opinions on breeding advice, was overstepping the bounds set out in the original agreement:

> These experiments, if so they can be called, have been carried out no more scientifically than were those of long ago under the rough-ready systems of Chas. Goodnight and Buffalo Jones...It appears that we occupy a somewhat invidious position in this matter of the Cattalo experiment. We are responsible, so far as I understand it, for the general care and feeding only of this herd. Such being the case, I do not think our Superintendent should proffer advice as to the technical and expert questions of matings etc., because, as copies of his letters are sent to Head Office we are responsible for his acts and advice, while at the same time we are precluded from advising what steps should be taken in regard to such questions as he now trenches upon.[45]

The trials themselves also faced several setbacks. The most serious was the problem of infertility. By 1925, none of the animals from the Boyd herd had produced any offspring. G. B. Rothwell, Dominion animal husbandman, wrote, "Every effort has been put forth toward the increase of this herd, all combinations of sires have been used, females have been subject to regular examination and treatment by veterinarians expert in the treatment of abnormal genital conditions. In spite of these efforts, no increase has been obtained from the original herd."[46] It was not known why the Boyd herd was infertile.[47] One of the main reasons for purchasing the herd was to avoid the obstacles and expense involved in the initial stages of the experiment, but the Department of Agriculture and the Parks Branch were forced to start again from scratch and they encountered all the obstacles with the first cross that they had hoped to avoid. The bison male and domestic female cross resulted in a high number of calves that were either aborted or stillborn. The cause of these deaths was attributed to an excessive amount of amniotic fluid. It was called the violent cross because the cows often succumbed as well.[48] Because of the high incidence of mortality among the cows, however, they discontinued the bison sire and domestic cow cross in favour of the domestic sire and bison cow cross, with which the Dominion government had more success.[49]

While females were common from a first cross and were found to be fertile when crossed with a pureblood bison or domestic bull,[50] male infertility was a problem that the experiment was never able to overcome. A report in 1955 stated that no fertile bulls resulting from the first cross were ever found.[51] Sterility among males from subsequent crosses was also high. The method followed was to cross the fertile heifers resulting from the first cross and subsequent crosses until a fertile bull was obtained. However, often 7/8 domestic males and occasionally 15/16 domestic males were still found to be sterile.[52] This setback proved to be a huge problem in view of the fact that the success of the experiment hinged on fertility of both the males and females.

The problem with infertility among the male hybrids was the main reason that yak were introduced into the experiment. Maxwell Graham, in agreement with R. I. Pocock, curator of mammals at the Regent's Park Zoological Collection in London, believed yak, an animal native to Tibet, to be an intermediate species between bison and domestic cattle.[53] Rocky Mountains Park had a yak herd on display, and so it was arranged to have some shipped to Buffalo National Park for use in the experiment. In June 1919, two cows, two bulls, and a bull calf were transferred to Buffalo National Park.[54]

The yak had no desirable features and they were only added to the experiment to counteract sterility of the male hybrids.[55] The objective was to "develop males carrying a maximum of Bison and a minimum of Yak blood, that [would] prove fertile and preponent when crossed on Domestic range cattle."[56] In 1923, the park began to see some results from its experiments in hybridizing yak: five heifers and one bull from a yak bull–domestic cow cross, two heifers from a bison bull–domestic cow cross, and one heifer from a yak bull–bison cow cross.[57] Initially, this new scheme seemed to be making headway, and in 1927, a *Maclean's* article entitled "Evolving the Arctic Cow" boasted of the strides being made towards developing a cattle breed for the Dominion's more northerly climates.[58] In 1928, however, it was decided to discontinue experimenting with yak. With the exception of a few hybrid females, the program returned to crossing only bison and domestic cattle because the yak was not considered to have added anything valuable to the experiment.[59] It is interesting that the introduction of yak into the breeding scenario was never considered an intrusion of non-indigenous species; not until 1937 did Superintendent A. G. Smith express the opinion that the yak should be removed from the park as only native animals should be found in national parks.[60]

While there had been no objections to moving the cattalo experiment to Buffalo National Park, there was much debate within the Parks Branch and between this branch and the Department of Agriculture over the risk that the cattalo experiment posed to the bison in terms of introducing disease. By the 1920s, it was clear that the bison preservation effort at Wainwright was being seriously compromised by the presence of tuberculosis. While there was no evidence of how tuberculosis was introduced into the Wainwright park, it is unlikely that the cattalo experiment was the source, as the first case of tuberculosis at Buffalo National Park was confirmed just before the cattalo herd arrived in Wainwright on 30 December 1916.[61]

While there is no way to determine if, or the extent to which, disease was spread by the introduction of the cattalo experiment, in hindsight, the diseased state of the bison herd also posed a great risk to the experiment. Much, however, can be learned about the perceptions of disease at this time through the debates between government officials in the Parks Branch and Department of Agriculture over relocating the cattalo experiment inside Buffalo National Park.

Two people who had serious reservations about moving the experiment to the park because of the danger it posed to the health of the bison herd were C. Gordon Hewitt, the Dominion entomologist, and Maxwell Graham, Chief of Park Animals. In 1916, Hewitt gave a very stern warning about locating the cattalo experiment to Buffalo National Park:

> In connection with the proposed experiments on the crossing of the buffalo and domestic cattle I would call your attention to the great importance of taking every precaution to prevent contact between the domestic cattle used in these experiments and the buffalo range. The enclosure in which the buffalo and cattle used in these experiments should, in my opinion, be separated by a double fence from the regular

buffalo range, with a considerable interval between, to avoid not only direct contact but the...possibility of the transference of organic material of any kind from the enclosure to the range. If such precautions are not taken an outbreak of disease among the domestic cattle might result in the decimation of the buffalo, which like all wild animals, are exceptionally susceptible to diseases of domestic animals.[62]

Although Graham was very much in favour of the experiments, he also expressed concern over moving the cattalo experiment to Wainwright. He granted there was always a certain risk for introduction of disease from outside Buffalo National Park, but felt that the introduction of the animals from Ontario posed an even greater risk, especially since they could be carriers of disease from other herds even if immune themselves. He warned, "I now desire to point out that if such action is taken, the herd of bison, now over 2,000 in number at Buffalo Park, will incur considerable additional risk of becoming infected with some variety of infectious disease." Then, in a prophetic warning he stated, "I would also point out that when an infectious disease is once brought into a large herd, the losses become very high, because it is difficult, if not impossible, to check it after it has once obtained a foothold." He strongly recommended that another area be set aside for the experiment.[63]

It is clear that J. H. Grisdale, director of Experimental Farms, did not take the warnings about the spread of disease seriously. In reference to Graham's objections about placing the cattalo experiment in Buffalo National Park, Grisdale argued that the arrangement to continue the experiments had been contingent on the availability of land in the park. In a letter to Harkin he wrote, "if it had not been agreed that the herd was destined for Wainwright, to occupy an enclosed portion of the Buffalo Park there, we would not have arranged for its purchase." He continued, "I am of the opinion that the objections raised to the arrangement agreed upon are not really very serious."[64]

Grisdale questioned some of the precautionary measures that had been recommended. He did not see the need to separate the cattalo enclosure from the main bison herd with a double fence when the park itself was only separated from the land outside by a single fence. He also did not consider the cattalo herd any more of a threat than livestock outside the park borders. He stated that all the cattalo had been tested for tuberculosis and any cattle introduced to the experiment would be accompanied by careful quarantine and testing. He had discussed concerns of the cattalo transmitting disease to the Wainwright bison with the veterinary director general and the pathologist of the Department of Agriculture and both assured him that the risk was practically negligible.[65]

Graham's request for an alternative location for the experiment was ignored. It seems that since the Department of Agriculture had already purchased the herd, plans were already set in motion. They did observe the precautions recommended by Hewitt to protect against the introduction of disease when they built the cattalo enclosure. For example, a double fence was installed around the entire enclosure with a width of 200 feet between the fences.[66] However, all the measures to ensure that the bison herd was protected from the cattalo were negated when the herd was moved to Wainwright before the area was ready for them. They arrived from Scott, Saskatchewan on the 30 December 1916 and were held in a temporary quarters until January 1918, when the cattalo enclosure was completed.[67] Further, the temporary enclosure appears to have been separated from the bison herd in the main park by only one fence; on 24 September 1917, a rider recorded in his diary that the gate to the enclosure had been broken by cattalo and bison fighting. Only seventeen of nineteen cattalo were accounted for. Harkin inferred from this and a second diary entry that two cattalo, one a bull, had escaped into the main park.[68] Furthermore, some of the cattalo were also in contact with other animals in the Visitor's Paddock where they were displayed during the summer months. In the winter, they were moved back to the cattalo paddock.[69]

The reaction to the escape of the cattalo into the main park best illustrates the park's priorities. When informed of the event, Harkin was concerned that the cattalo bull might breed with some of the bison, especially since the escape occurred during breeding season.[70] This concern suggests that the department did have an interest in maintaining the integrity of the plains bison outside the confines of the cattalo experiment. The escaped cattalo, however, may not have posed much of a threat to the composition of the herd. A number of hybrids existed among the Pablo bison when the Dominion government purchased the herd. Warden Bud Cotton recalled some of the original Montana bison having domestic characteristics. "Lizzie was a lady from the hills of Montana, all buffalo in shape with a beautiful coat of rich, dark brown hair, but showing the strain of her renegade domestic dad in a big Roman nose and light brown eyes."[71] He also remembered:

> One outstanding family group—twenty-one head—we christened the
> Brindles or Ambers. Mother had been shipped in from the Flathead

Reservation and raised her family in the Buffalo Reserve. They were all true buffalo as to shape and size, but distinctly marked with brindle stripes (tiger fashion) which showed beautiful hides. Horns and hoofs were pure amber color. These hides were in great demand, so every roundup any of the strain showing up were cut out for beef and hide.

When the old cow checked in her chips to the hide hunters, the brindle strain disappeared too. Thus, we lost a grand old lady buffalo with a hidden past.[72]

In 1918, when it was reported that a hybrid cow and her progeny were still roaming in the park, Maxwell Graham responded, "I am surprised to learn that any hybrids are still to be found in our main herd, as very shortly after the creation of this Branch explicit instructions were given to cut out all such [animals], and I remember that not only was this reported as having been done but reports were also received from the Pat Burns Co., praising very highly the beef qualities of these hybrids....If any hybrids are still to be found in our herd at Buffalo Park, these should be cut out and placed in the new Cattalo enclosure."[73] However, as late as 1923, Seymour Hadwen, pathologist, found that several animals still exhibited characteristics that were not true to the plains bison:

> There are several animals which have yellowish or ambered coloured horns which are not quite the same shape as the typical buffalo. These animals have a quite definite brindling of the hair, especially over the back and shoulders. Darker stripes can be seen running almost circularly around the body and are very much like those one sees in a brindle cow. These animals possibly hark back to some cross with cattle. Another very noticeable difference is in the black line which runs from the hump to the top of the head; it varies very much in width and darkness. If the herd is to be cut down, it would seem desirable to try and eliminate all these animals which do not appear to be running true to type.[74]

Harkin should have been concerned about the potential spread of disease posed by the escaped cattalo. However, this concern was not even mentioned, perhaps because the cattalo herd was considered to be disease-free. Grisdale confirmed the animals had been tested for tuberculosis before they were moved.[75] However, given that by this time tuberculosis had been discovered in at least one bison in the park herd and was suspected in many others, it is puzzling that there was no concern that the main bison herd might pose a threat to the experiment.

Once the cattalo herd had been moved to its new enclosure, the trials themselves took precedence over the precautionary measures first adhered to. The cattalo herd was not breeding and Caretaker James Wilson thought it might be because the animals were too heavy. He suggested that if the cattalo were kept in a smaller enclosure they would lose some weight and the situation might improve. A. G. Smith wrote to E. S. Archibald, offering Wilson's proposal that an area between the double fences of the cattalo enclosure be fenced off for this purpose.[76] The lack of concern over the potential threat of the spread of disease is apparent in the willingness of those in authority at both the Parks Branch and the Department of Agriculture to bend the very guidelines they had established for protecting the main bison herd. Harkin, while restating the importance of the fence to protect against the transference of disease, initially consented to the request. In response to Archibald he wrote:

> If there is no other way of overcoming the difficulty which Mr. Wilson's proposal suggests and you could guarantee that no animal which is in the enclosure now or will be in the future, so long as the lane is being utilized in the way suggested, has any communicable disease such a guarantee from you would be sufficient to satisfy me that the health of the buffalo would not be seriously menaced by such a procedure.[77]

While Harkin was willing to compromise, he certainly showed more concern about the potential transference of disease than E. S. Archibald, Director of Experimental Farms. In response to Harkin he wrote:

> While we know of no disease whatever existing or having ever existed in our Cattalo, and think the chance of any such trouble developing are almost negligible, I am afraid it is impossible for any one to give such a guarantee as you suggest and, such being the case, if this is your final decision, and you really cannot see your way to run what would seem to be a very remote risk, we shall have to try and make some other arrangements.[78]

In the end, Harkin informed Archibald that he was not willing to run the risk of using the laneway for a cattalo pen. Yet, it is unclear if Archibald received Harkin's instructions because the letter Harkin wrote to him was never sent.[79]

While it does not seem that tuberculosis was as rampant in the cattalo herd, the disease was eventually found among the cattalo after they moved

A Department of the Interior map showing the ranges of the northern and southern wood bison herds. The plains bison herd from Wainwright was introduced into the southern range as it was believed the two herds would not mix.

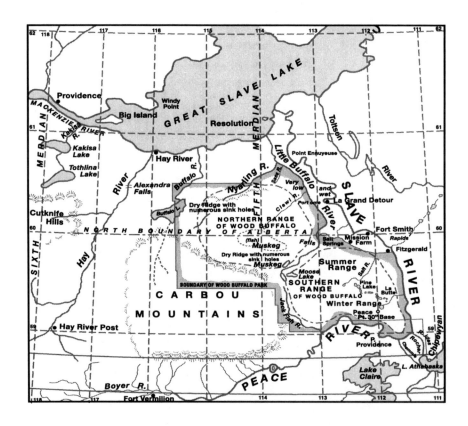

to the park. In November 1917, local veterinarian S. E. Wiley examined a seven-year-old cattalo bull, Port Royal, which was in poor condition and anaemic. Although he was unable to make a definite diagnosis, he suspected tuberculosis since the animal had been gradually deteriorating in health for some time and the other animals were in excellent condition. He recommended that a tuberculosis test be given, but it is unclear if this test was performed.[80] By 1924, a cattalo cow was sent with two bison calves to the research station in Lethbridge for experimental purposes because she had reacted to the tuberculosis test and then needed to be disposed of.[81]

In many ways, the transfer of the plains bison north to Wood Buffalo National Park to alleviate the pressure of overpopulation at the Wainwright park paralleled the decision to relocate the cattalo experiment to Wainwright. Both involved the issues of hybridization between two species and the transference of disease. However, the debate surrounding the transfer of plains bison north proceeded quite differently. When the cattalo experiment was moved to Wainwright, there was absolutely no debate over how conducting a crossbreeding experiment in a national park would violate the bison-saving effort and the debate over the potential threat the experiment posed in terms of spreading disease remained within the government circles. Yet when the move to Wood Buffalo Park was publicized, most opposition arose from the public sphere and any opposition that arose in government circles was suppressed. Naturalists and zoologists took issue with the transfer because they believed that the plains bison would both interbreed with the wood bison, obliterating the latter species, and spread tuberculosis to this disease-free herd. Clearly, the Parks Branch had learned little in terms of the potential risks from the experience with the cattalo experiment. Literally no precaution was taken to ensure that the wood bison would be protected from the plains bison. This careless attitude pointed to a deeper crisis: the overpopulation problem. The Parks Branch had been trying to reduce the bison through slaughter, but this method was expensive and they were not realizing any revenue through the sale of the bison products. The decision to send the bison north was made because it was the fastest and most economical way to relieve the pressure on the Wainwright range. The threat that the plains bison posed to the wood bison was secondary to the problems that Buffalo National Park was facing.

The scheme of shipping excess bison to the habitat of the wood bison in the north, first raised by Maxwell Graham in September 1919, was introduced again by H. E. Sibbald, Dominion Parks Inspector, in 1923.[82] Not long after, W. W. Cory, Deputy Minister of the Department of the Interior, echoed Sibbald's suggestion stating that instead of slaughtering the bison, it might be a good idea to transfer healthy stock to Wood Buffalo National Park.[83] He called a conference on 30 May 1923 to discuss the proposal. Present at the meeting were O. S. Finnie, Director of the North West Territories, J. B. Harkin, Commissioner of National Parks, Dr. Frederick Torrance, Veterinary Director General for the Department of Agriculture, and Superintendent A. G. Smith. Cory also acted as Commissioner of the North West Territories.[84] Although the tubercular state of the herd was given some attention at the meeting, it was clear that it was not considered serious. Cory asked Torrance for his opinion on whether the Wainwright bison could recover from tuberculosis if transplanted to the Fort Smith area, and whether this move would jeopardize the wood bison. Torrance stated that although some improvement might be noted in less advanced cases, the relocation of such a large number of diseased animals into an area with a herd that was not infected would be extremely hazardous. It is not known whether the potential danger that the two species would interbreed was discussed at this initial meeting. In the end, it seems that the group opted to transplant the bison in a manner which posed the least danger to the wood bison: only young animals should be selected for transport, and the animals would have to pass a tuberculosis test before being shipped north.[85]

On the same day of the meeting called by W. W. Cory, Torrance, perhaps not happy with the final decision, wrote a letter to the Parks Branch and stated his opinion on moving the younger bison north: "This proposition is objectionable from a health point of view, in that it would be almost certain to carry infection to this herd of wood buffalo, which presumably is at present free from this disease."[86] However, even with this objection, Torrance left the door open for the Parks Branch by suggesting that, "If this proposition were, however, modified and preparation made so that young animals up to the age of yearlings only were transferred, and that these animals were previous to transference submitted to the tuberculin test, so as to eliminate any that reacted, much of the objection would be removed."[87] He suggested that his branch, the Department of Agriculture, make arrangements for the planning of the necessary enclosures and squeezes and the delivery of the tests.[88]

That Maxwell Graham was the first to suggest the Parks Branch move the bison north to the habitat of the wood bison is surprising given that he knew that the Wainwright herd had tuberculosis and that he had been dead set against relocating the cattalo experiment to Wainwright because of the potential threat of disease. He was not in attendance at the conference and he was no longer with the Parks Branch when the transfer decision was made.[89] In 1922, he had taken on a new role as Chief of the Wild Life Division. Nonetheless, in the December 1924 issue of the *Canadian Field-Naturalist*, Graham continued to endorse the proposal of Wood Buffalo Park as the new outlet for the surplus plains bison. Graham, knowing the health status of the Wainwright herd, made no mention of tuberculosis at all in his article,[90] yet it is clear he knew the dangers that the disease posed. In a 1919 memorandum, he outlined the symptoms and spread of the disease and issued a stern warning that bison exhibiting such symptoms or reacting to a tuberculin test should be slaughtered.[91]

Historian John Sandlos shows that Graham was a key proponent of the transfer program. Amazingly, he was able to "dismiss the opinions of leading zoologists, misrepresent the views of his colleagues and ignore expert advice he had received from within the civil service"[92] despite the fact that he seemed to have knowledge of the danger that the transfer posed. Sandlos cites an internal 1923 memorandum that shows that Graham acknowledged that the risk of infecting the wood bison with tuberculosis was great. To O. S. Finnie he wrote:

> It would seem therefore in Doctor Torrance's opinion we must face a certain risk of infection from the introduction of even young, tested, buffalo coming from the infected herd at Wainwright...Since Dr. Torrance has given his opinion it is hardly proper for me to say more on the matter of possible infection.[93]

Sandlos argues that, for Graham, the practicality of the project outweighed the risks.[94] Perhaps the very fact that Graham did not mention tuberculosis in his article indicates that he had some issue with the danger the transfer posed in this regard. However, given that he was no longer with the Parks Branch, perhaps he believed his opinion would have little influence.

While Graham may have had issue with the transfer of a diseased plains bison herd, he showed no serious objection to plains and wood bison interbreeding. In fact, he did not consider the two types of bison to be separate species. Rather, he believed the wood bison, the last wild bison in North America, were and "the finest specimens of their species, superior in pelage, size, and vigour to those of the plains."[95] Any difference between the plains and wood bison Graham attributed to the environment they were living in.[96] To him, the pure wood bison serve a very useful purpose for the parks system.

"The time is approaching" he stated, "when an infusion of new unrelated blood will be needed by our herds in the National parks, and it is only from the northern herds that such infusion can be obtained."[97]

Given his belief that the wood bison were a purer version of the plains bison and needed to be safeguarded for future use in the national parks system, it is curious that Graham supported a proposal to move a diseased and (what he considered) inferior herd into the wood bison habitat. However, he did not believe that moving the plains bison north would endanger or obliterate the entire wood bison population. There were two ranges for these northern bison, containing two separate herds, which supposedly did not mingle with each other. Graham argued, "Since it is into the southern range only that it is proposed to introduce plains bison from the Wainwright Park, in which range some 1,000 wood-bison are at present established, those bison indigenous to the northern range...will remain inviolate so far as admixture with the introduced bison is concerned."[98]

Not everyone accepted Graham's argument. Francis Harper of Cornell University (previously of the Bureau of Biological Survey, Washington, D.C.), using Harry V. Radford's findings, argued that the two types of bison had distinct characteristics.[99] He stated, "Interbreeding will undoubtedly take place, and with the introduced Plains Buffalo vastly in the majority, the descendants a few generations hence will naturally have more of the characteristics of the latter than the Wood Buffalo."[100] He argued that there was no evidence that the northern and southern herds would not mix, because there was no physical barrier preventing contact between the two herds. Thus, there was also a potential for disease to spread.[101] Others, like the American Society of Mammalogists, expressed their disapproval of the transfer in subsequent issues of *Canadian Field-Naturalist*. Naturalist W. E. Saunders from London, Ontario, argued:

> There are so many examples the world over, of calamitous results arising from the interference of man with native fauna, that one can only suppose that the promoters of this scheme to mix the blood of the two Buffalo, have not sought advice from any student of Natural Science...it would be better to lose the whole Wainwright herd, rather than risk the last remnant of the Wood Buffalo.[102]

William Hornaday, vice-president of the American Bison Society and president of the New York Zoological Park, also raised objections to the move when he learned the Wainwright herd was diseased. He was greatly shocked to hear that the bison had tuberculosis. In a letter to Francis Harper he stated, "If it is as bad as your informant states—which I certainly hope it is not— then the conditions are indeed terrible. I had not before heard even a whisper to the effect that tuberculosis had found lodgement in the great Canadian herd."[103] He considered the proposal to move bison north a fatal mistake, but admitted that there was really nothing anyone outside Canada could do without it being seen as interference.[104]

There was also some dissent inside government circles, as was made apparent in a dispute that involved Hoyes Lloyd and Harrison Lewis, Supervisor of Wildlife Protection for the Parks Branch and the Chief Federal Migratory Bird Officer, respectively. Both men were involved with the Ottawa Field Naturalist's Club: Lloyd was president and Lewis was editor of *Canadian Field-Naturalist*. At the 28 February 1925 club meeting, it was decided to send a copy of Harper's letter from the February 1925 issue of *Canadian Field-Naturalist* to the Minister of the Interior accompanied by a letter from the club endorsing Harper's position that plains bison should not be sent north. The outcome of the incident is proof that the government indeed had knowledge of the potential danger in which it was placing wood bison. It also verifies how volatile the proposal had become; the government was not willing to countenance public servants breaking rank. Lloyd and Lewis were informed that they could either resign from the Field Naturalist's Club or be expelled from the Department of the Interior. Both resigned their positions at the club.[105] Years later, Dr. Lewis told W. F. Lothian that the ultimatum was not conveyed by letter or memorandum, but came by the grapevine from the deputy minister's office.[106]

The decision to send bison north was not changed by the protests; plains bison were shipped north over a period of four years. As had been the case with the cattalo experiment, initial regulations set out to protect the wood bison were compromised. For one, a decision was made to dispense with the tuberculin test since only young bison, one- and two-year-olds, were to be shipped. Initially these young bison were chosen because it was thought that they posed little risk of spreading disease.[107] It is likely that evidence from the 1923 slaughter influenced this decision. All nine of the spring calves killed were free from the disease, and only one of twelve yearlings slaughtered was found to be slightly infected.[108] In his January 1924 report to the veterinary director general, Waddy stated that while the older cows and bulls had "extreme prevailence [sic] of generalized tuberculosis," the bison under the age of five that had been slaughtered in the past few days had been found to be free from the disease.[109] Thus, it appears none of the animals sent north were tested for tuberculosis.[110]

Even the policy of sending young bison north was not strictly adhered to, however. When 2,000 bison were rounded up for the transfer in the 1925 season, a number of cows formed a part of this group. O. S. Finnie wired A. G. Smith and stated, "Positively no buffalo over two years can be shipped."[111] The ratio agreed upon in 1924 had been one male to five females among the yearlings; no two-year-old males were to be shipped. In 1925, the department approved a sex ratio of one male to two females for both yearlings and two-year olds. Finnie considered the male portion proposed for the 1926 shipment, one male to one female for the yearlings and 450 males to 250 females for the two-year olds, excessive and advised that they allow three-year-old females to be added in order to supplement the sex ratio.[112] Although it does not appear that any three-year olds were shipped, Warden Ray Sharp recalled that in the last two years, 1927 and 1928, they did not adhere to any ratio; they had to ship anything of the yearlings and two-year-olds in order to get the numbers.[113]

In 1932, one of the most scathing comments regarding the transfer of the bison north was made by Thomas Barbour, director of the Museum of Comparative Zoology at Harvard University. In a review for the magazine *Science* of the book *Wild Beasts Today* written by Harold Shepstone[114] Barbour stated,

> This, one of the most tragic examples of bureaucratic stupidity in all history, was done against the protests of both Canadian and American naturalists who would rather have seen the surplus bison killed. They were known to be infected with bovine tuberculosis and they are certain to interbreed as well as infect the wood bison, which is a far finer animal and one of great zoological interest ....The book would have done well to have shown up this transfer to the public in its true light as a real tragedy and not as a triumph of conservation.[115]

In response to the review, J. D. Soper, chief federal wildlife officer of the Canadian Wildlife Service for the Prairie Provinces, confirmed that there had been merit in the warnings given by the naturalists and zoologists:

> It is true that the "Wainwrights" were and are still infected with bovine tuberculosis. There can scarcely be any doubt that these animals are interbreeding and infecting the wood bison at the present time; the "Wainwrights" are drifting everywhere and occupying the former

range of the "originals". The two races have already intermingled to a great extent and almost without question are transmitting tuberculosis one to the other. There are now reports that the "Wainwrights" have even invaded what we have regarded as the "remote northern area" of the park.[116]

According to park employees at Wood Buffalo National Park, the plains bison herd mingled with the wood bison almost immediately after arriving at the park. William A. Fuller, a mammalogist employed in the Dominion Wildlife Service (later the Canadian Wildlife Service) wrote that in 1950 a professional butcher and a veterinary meat inspector were brought to Wood Buffalo National Park for the annual bison hunt. Fuller worked with the veterinarian and learned how to inspect the animals for tuberculosis. With this knowledge, he continued to inspect bison in the annual kills and his findings revealed that the disease had spread. He gives figures for the incidence of tuberculosis found among the herd from 1952 to 1956: three-quarters of adult and old males tested positive for tuberculosis. On the whole, 38 per cent of males and 40 per cent of females were found to have the disease.[117]

The lack of judgement displayed by members of the government and the Parks Branch over the introduction of the cattalo experiment and the shipping of plains bison north to Wood Buffalo National Park had far-reaching consequences. The hybridization experiment was certainly a product of the early 20th century and another way to make the bison herd at Wainwright useful. The decision to move the cattalo experiment to Wainwright, however, contradicted the bison-saving effort in principle and set a bad precedent. The involvement of the Parks Branch in this experimental work may explain their apathy towards the decision to introduce the plains bison, a distinct species, into the habitat of the wood bison.

There is no excuse for the Parks Branch's blatant disregard of the issue of the spread of disease. Zoologists and naturalists voiced their objections regarding the transfer of plains bison north and informed the government of its obligation to the preservation of the wood bison. The Park Branch's decision to ignore protests raises the question of whether the decision makers had any preservationist ethic at all. The fact that they quashed objections by those within the government circles is proof that the government's main interest was not the plains bison but rather eliminating its overpopulation burden by removing the problem to a remote area. This quick fix, however, was disastrous. The plains bison interbred and spread disease to the wood bison and the ripple effect from this decision is still felt today.

1. Cattalo are the progeny resulting from a cross between bison and domestic cattle. While Mossom Boyd, the hybrid experimenter from Bobcaygeon, Ontario, reserved this title for offspring from parents that were mixed blood, the term had also been used loosely to connote hybrids and descendants from one pure parent. LAC, Commissioner to Edmund Seymour, 4 Jul. 1917, Parks Canada Files, BNP, RG 84, Vol. 52, BU233, pt. 1; Jorgen Nelson, "How Practical Are Cattalo? Buffalos and Domestic Cattle Have Long Been Crossbred," *American Feed and Grain Dealer* 30 (Sept. 1946), 8.

2. For example, the German government was carrying out experiments in crossing the zebu with domestic cattle to create an animal that would be immune to the tsetse fly, and the Department of Agriculture in Russia was experimenting with crossing Russian cattle of the steppes with yak. LAC, W. W. Cory to G. F. O'Halloran, 2 Mar. 1914, Department of Agriculture Files, Cattalo, RG 17, Vol. 1249, 245817.

3. A. Deakin, G. W. Muir, and A. G. Smith, *Hybridization of Domestic Cattle, Bison and Yak* (Ottawa 1935), 5 and Nelson, "How Practical Are Cattalo?" 9.

4. For example, hybrids occurred in the herds of Frederick Dupree and James McKay and Charles Alloway. Coder, "National Movement," 5, 25.

5. Whealdon et al., *I Will Be Meat for My Salish*, 118.

6. Whealdon et al., *I Will Be Meat for My Salish*, 118. Some of their cattalo would have come from C. "Buffalo" Jones's stock. In 1893, Pablo and Allard purchased from Jones eighteen hybrid bison and twenty-six purebred bison. Coder, "The National Movement," 39.

7. Nelson, "How Practical Are Cattalo?" 9.

8. C. J. Jones, "My Buffalo Experiments," *Independent* 60 (1906), 1355.

9. George Bird Grinnell, "The Last of the Buffalo," *Scribner's Magazine* 12 (Sept. 1892), 274.

10. Jones, "My Buffalo Experiments," 1355.

11. *Goodnight's American Buffalo Ranch, Goodnight Texas* (Dallas 1910), 2, 3.

12. Charles Goodnight, "My Experience with Bison Hybrids," *Journal of Heredity* 5 (1914), 199.

13. LAC, C. J.(Buffalo)Jones to J. B. Harkin, 14 Jul. 1917, Parks Canada Files, BNP, RG 84, Vol. 52, BU233, pt. 1.

14. Colpitts states that thirteen bison were purchased in 1878. Colpitts, *Game in the Garden*, 58. Coder, however, uses Bedson's own statement that eight bison were purchased. Bedson made this statement eight years after the bison had been purchased. Coder, "National Movement," 5, 49.

15. Colpitts, *Game in the Garden*, 55–57.

16. Thompson, "A List of the Mammals of Manitoba," 11. This appears to be Ernest Thompson Seton. Colpitts, *Game in the Garden*, 58.

17. Colpitts, *Game in the Garden*, 58–60.

18. LAC, Maxwell Graham to J. B. Harkin, 30 Nov. 1912, Department of Agriculture Files, Cattalo, RG 17, Vol. 1249, 245817.

19. LAC, Howard Douglas to Commissioner, 14 [Feb.] 1912, Parks Canada Files, BNP, RG 84, Vol. 52, BU233, pt. 1.

20. LAC, Mossom Boyd, "A Short Account of the Experiment of Crossing the American Bison with Domestic Cattle," n.d., Department of Agriculture Files, Cattalo, RG 17, Vol. 1249, 245817.

21. LAC, G. Cust Boyd to Martin Burrell, 21 Jul. 1914, Department of Agriculture Files, Cattalo, RG 17, Vol. 1249, 245817.

22. LAC, Boyd, "Crossing Bison and Cattle," 189; J. B. Harkin to Edmund Seymour, 4 Jul. 1917, Parks Canada Files, BNP, RG 84, Vol. 52, BU233, pt. 1.

23. LAC, Howard Douglas to J. B. Harkin, 14 [Feb.] 1912, Parks Canada Files, BNP, RG 84, Vol. 52, BU233, pt. 1.

24. LAC, Howard Douglas to James A. Smart, 15 Oct. 1903, Parks Canada Files, BNP, RG 84, Vol. 52, BU233, pt. 1.

25. LAC, F. H. Byshe to Mr. Harkin, 12 Dec. 1911, Parks Canada Files, BNP, RG 84, Vol. 52, BU233, pt. 1.

26. LAC, Howard Douglas to A. B. MacDonald, 3 Feb. 1912 and Howard Douglas to Commissioner, 7 Feb. 1912, Parks Canada Files, BNP, RG 84, Vol. 52, BU233, pt. 1.

27. LAC, Howard Douglas to Commissioner, 7 Feb. 1912, Parks Canada Files, BNP, RG 84, Vol. 52, BU233, pt. 1.

28. LAC, J. B. Harkin to Mr. Cory, 27 Jan. 1912, Parks Canada Files, BNP, RG 84, Vol. 52, BU233, pt. 1.

29. LAC, Memorandum to Mr. Mitchell, 29 Apr. 1918, Parks Canada Files, BNP, RG 84, Vol. 982, BU2[548608], pt. 2.

30. LAC, W. W. Cory to G. F. O'Halloran, 2 Mar. 1914, Department of Agriculture Files, Cattalo, RG 17, Vol. 1249, 245817; LAC, J. B. Harkin to Mr. Cory, 27 Jan. 1912 and J. B. Harkin to Mr. Cory, 11 Dec. 1912, Parks Canada Files, BNP, RG 84, Vol. 52, BU233, pt. 1.

31. LAC, Maxwell Graham to Mr. Harkin, 30 Nov. 1912, Parks Canada Files, BNP, RG 84, Vol. 52, BU233, pt. 1.

32. LAC, E. S. Archibald, Memo Re: Buffalo Cattle Hybrids on the Estate of M. M. Boyd, Bobcaygeon, Ont., 18 Jun. 1915, Department of Agriculture Files, Cattalo, RG 17, Vol. 1249, 245817.

33. LAC, Note from Maxwell Graham, 25 Jul. 1914, Parks Canada Files, BNP, RG 84, Vol. 52, BU233, pt. 1; LAC, Heaton's Agency to Martin Burrell, 22 Jul. 1914, G. Cust Boyd to Martin Burrell, 21 Jul. 1914, Department of Agriculture Files, Cattalo, RG 17, Vol. 1249, 245817.

34. LAC, J. H. Grisdale to Deputy Minister, Department of Agriculture, 31 Aug. 1914, E. S. Archibald, Memo. re Buffalo Cattle Hybrids on the Estate of M. M. Boyd, Bobcaygeon, Ont., 18 Jun. 1915, Memo. re Cattalo, 5 Jan. 1916, Department of Agriculture Files, Cattalo, RG 17, Vol. 1249, 245817.

35. LAC, Commissioner to E. S. Archibald, 3 Dec. 1915, Parks Canada Files, BNP, RG 84, Vol. 52, BU233, pt. 1; LAC, Memo. re: Cattalo, 5 Jan. 1916, Department of Agriculture Files, Cattalo, RG 17, Vol. 1249, 245817.

36. LAC, J. H. Grisdale, to George F. O'Halloran, 11 May 1914, Department of Agriculture Files, Cattalo, RG 17, Vol. 1249, 245817.

37. LAC, E. S. Archibald, Memo. re: Buffalo Cattle Hybrids, 18 Jun. 1915, Department of Agriculture Files, Cattalo, RG 17, Vol. 1249, 245817.

38. LAC, J. H. Grisdale to Deputy Minister, Department of Agriculture, 31 Aug. 1914, Department of Agriculture Files, Cattalo, RG 17, Vol. 1249, 245817. Up to this point, it appears that trials at the experimental farms had more to do with feeding experiments. LAC, J. H. Grisdale to Mr. O'Halloran, 13 Sept. 1915, Department of Agriculture Files, Cattalo, RG 17, Vol. 1249, 245817.

39. LAC, A. G. Smith to E. Hunter, 10 Mar. 1920, Parks Canada Files, BNP, RG 84, Vol. 54, BU233, pt. 2.

40. LAC, A. G. Smith to E. S. Archibald, 10 May 1920, Parks Canada Files, BNP, RG 84, Vol. 54, BU233, pt. 2.

41. LAC, Director of Park Animals to E. S Archibald, 4 Jul. 1921, Parks Canada Files, BNP, RG 84, Vol. 54, BU233, pt. 2; LAC, J. H. Grisdale to J. B. Harkin, 29 Oct. 1917 and A.G. Smith to Director, Experimental Farms, 16 Nov. 1917, Parks Canada Files, BNP, RG 84, Vol. 52, BU233, pt. 1; LAC, E. S. Hopkins to Dr. Barton, 20 Nov. 1939, Department of Agriculture Files, Cattalo, RG 17, Vol. 3456, 30-9-1(1).

42. LAC, A. G. Smith to Commissioner, 22 Feb. 1918, Parks Canada Files, BNP, RG 84, Vol. 52, BU233, pt. 1.

43. LAC, A. G. Smith to E. S. Archibald, 24 Mar. 1920, E. S. Archibald to J. B. Harkin, 15 May 1920, and A. G. Smith to E. S. Archibald, 27 May 1920, Parks Canada Files, BNP, RG 84, Vol. 54, BU233, pt. 2.

44. LAC, Maxwell Graham to Commissioner, 1 Mar. 1918, Parks Canada Files, BNP, RG 84, Vol. 52, BU233, pt. 1.

45. G. B. Rothwell, *Report of the Dominion Animal Husbandman for the Year Ending March 31, 1924* (Ottawa 1925), 57.

46. The problems associated with the successful breeding of the Boyd herd were attributed to the infertility of the males and to the combined effects of the increasing age of the females, their continually open state, genital abnormalities arising from these conditions, and the high condition of the females due to the good grazing in the enclosures. Rothwell, *Report of the Dominion Animal Husbandman*, 57. It was also suggested that constant moving of the herd (from Ontario to Saskatchewan to Wainwright and between enclosures once at the park) was a reason that the herd was not breeding. LAC, A. G. Smith to A. G. Sinclair, 21 Jan. 1919, Parks Canada Files, BNP, RG 84, Vol. 52, BU233, pt. 1.

47. Rothwell, *Report of the Dominion Animal Husbandman*, 56, 59.

48. Nelson, "How Practical Are Cattalo?" 9; LAC, E. S. Archibald to Dr. Grisdale, 29 Jun. 1928, Department of Agriculture Files, Cattalo, RG 17, Vol. 3456, 30-9-1(1).

49. Rothwell, *Report of the Dominion Animal Husbandman*, 56.

50. H. F. Peters, *Range Experimental Farm, Manyberries, Alberta, Progress Report, 1948–1953* (Ottawa 1955), 20.

51. Nelson, "How Practical Are Cattalo?" 9, 27.

52. LAC, Chief of the Animal Division to Commissioner, 15 Mar. 1918, Parks Canada Files, BNP, RG 84, Vol. 52, BU233, pt. 1.

53. LAC, J. M. Wardle to J. B. Harkin, 19 Jun. 1919, Parks Canada Files, BNP, RG 84, Vol. 52, BU233, pt. 1. Yak were first introduced into the national park system in 1909, when the Duke of Bedford presented a small herd to the Dominion government. LAC, E. S. Archibald, *The Yak in Canada*, n.d., Parks Canada Files, BNP, RG 84, Vol. 55, BU241, pt. 1.

54. LAC, "Cross Breeding Experiments at Buffalo Park, Wainwright, Alta," n.d., Parks Canada Files, BNP, RG 84, Vol. 54, BU233, pt. 2; LAC, E. S. Archibald to Dr. Grisdale, 22 Dec. 1923, Department of Agriculture Files, Cattalo, RG 17, Vol. 3456, 30-9-1(1).

55. LAC, "Cross Breeding Experiments at Buffalo Park, Wainwright, Alta," n.d., Parks Canada Files, BNP, RG 84, Vol. 54, BU233, pt. 2.

56. LAC, "Experimental Cross-Breeding of Bison (Buffalo) with Domestic Cattle, Yak, etc.," n.d., Parks Canada Files, BNP, RG 84, Vol. 54, BU233, pt. 2.

57. *MacLean's Magazine*, 15 Jan. 1927, 21, Alan N. Longstaff, "Evolving the Arctic Cow."

58. Deakin, Muir, and Smith, *Hybridization*, 27.

59. LAC, A. G. Smith to Controller, National Parks Bureau, 26 Oct. 1937, Parks Canada Files, BNP, RG 84, Vol. 55, BU241, pt. 1.

60. UAA, T.B. at Buffalo Park between Dec. 1916 to Jan. 1st, 1922, Buffalo National Park Files, 2002-18-4.

61. LAC, C. Gordon Hewitt to J. B. Harkin, 2 Feb. 1916, Parks Canada Files, BNP, RG 84, Vol. 52, BU233, pt. 1.

62. LAC, Chief of the Animal Division to J. B. Harkin, 27 Jun. 1916, Parks Canada Files, BNP, RG 84, Vol. 52, BU233, pt. 1.

63. UAA, J. H. Grisdale to J. B. Harkin, 5 Jul. 1916, Buffalo National Park Files, 2002-18-4.

64. UAA, J. H. Grisdale to J. B. Harkin, 5 Jul. 1916, Buffalo National Park Files, 2002-18-4.

65. LAC, E. S. Archibald to J. B. Harkin, 2 Jun. 1919 and Commissioner to E. S. Archibald, 9 Jun. 1919, Parks Canada Files, BNP, RG 84, Vol. 52, BU233, pt. 1.

66. LAC, A. G. Smith to Commissioner, 3 Jan. 1917 and A. G. Smith to Commissioner, 22 Feb. 1918, Parks Canada Files, BNP, RG 84, Vol. 52, BU233, pt. 1.

67. LAC, Commissioner to A. G. Smith, 5 Nov. 1917, Parks Canada Files, BNP, RG 84, Vol. 52, BU233, pt. 1. The cattalo herd consisted of only nineteen animals; one cow was destroyed shortly after arriving at the park. LAC, Maxwell Graham to J. B. Harkin, 22 Aug. 1917 and A. G. Smith to Commissioner, 18 Sept. 1917, Parks Canada Files, BNP, RG 84, Vol. 52, BU233, pt. 1.

68. *Home of the Buffalo*, VHS, with commentary by Ray Sharp (n.d., Battle River Historical Society). The Oct 12, 1927 entry in Davey Davison's diary reads, "I went to Mott Lake Enc. & put the 5 Cattalo into Petersens Enc & headed them south to the Cattalo Enc." BNPFA, Diary of Davey Davison, Jan. 1, 1927 to Jan. 2, 1928, Davison fonds.

69. LAC, Commissioner to Superintendent, Buffalo Park, 5 Nov. 1917, Parks Canada Files, BNP, RG 84, Vol. 52, BU233, pt. 1.

70. Cotton, *Buffalo Bud*, 107.

71. Cotton, *Buffalo Bud*, 107–108.

72. LAC, Chief of the Animal Division to Commissioner, 15 Mar. 1918, Parks Canada Files, BNP, RG 84, Vol. 52, BU233, pt. 1.

73. LAC, Seymour Hadwen to J. B. Harkin, 21 Feb. 1923, Parks Canada Files, BNP, RG 84, Vol. 58, BU299-2, pt. 1.

74. UAA, J. H. Grisdale to J. B. Harkin, 5 Jul. 1916, Buffalo National Park Files, 2002-18-4.

75. LAC, A. G. Smith to E. S. Archibald, 26 May 1919, Parks Canada Files, BNP, RG 84, Vol. 52, BU233, pt. 1.

76. LAC, Commissioner to E. S. Archibald, 9 Jun. 1919, Parks Canada Files, BNP, RG 84, Vol. 52, BU233, pt. 1.

77. LAC, E. S. Archibald to J. B. Harkin, 12 Jun. 1919, Parks Canada Files, BNP, RG 84, Vol. 52, BU233, pt. 1.

78. The letter was found in 1920 and believed to have been never sent. LAC, J. B. Harkin to E. S. Archibald, 17 Jun. 1919 and note, anonymous, n.d., Parks Canada Files, BNP, RG 84, Vol. 52, BU233, pt. 1.

79. LAC, S. E. Wiley to A. G. Smith, 3 Nov. 1917, and A. G. Smith to Commissioner, 7 Nov. 1917 and A. G. Smith to Director of Experimental Farms, 12 Sep. 1919, Parks Canada Files, BNP, RG 84, Vol. 52, BU233, pt. 1.

80. LAC, A. G. Smith to A. E. Cameron, 3 Dec. 1924, Parks Canada Files, BNP, RG 84, Vol. 58, BU299-2, pt. 1.

81. LAC, Maxwell Graham to J. B. Harkin, 29 Sept. 1919, Parks Canada Files, BNP, RG 84, Vol. 53, File BU232, pt. 1; LAC, H. E. Sibbald to J. B. Harkin, 17 Jan. 1923, Parks Canada Files, BNP, RG 84, Vol. 52, File BU232-1, pt. 1.

82. There had only been one small experimental slaughter by the time the transfer suggestion arose in 1923, perhaps proof that public opinion was also influential in the formation of this proposal.

83. UAA, Summary of correspondence dealing with the transfer of the buffalo from Wainwright to Wood Buffalo Park, 6 May 1933, Buffalo National Park Files, 2002-18-1.

84. UAA, Summary of correspondence dealing with the transfer of the buffalo from Wainwright to Wood Buffalo Park, 6 May 1933, Buffalo National Park Files, 2002-18-1.

85. LAC, Fred Torrance to W. W. Cory, 30 May 1923, Parks Canada Files, BNP, RG 84, Vol. 58, BU299-2, pt. 1.

86. LAC, Parks Canada Files, BNP, RG 84, Vol. 58, BU299-2, pt. 1.

87. LAC, Parks Canada Files, BNP, RG 84, Vol. 58, BU299-2, pt. 1.

88. W. A. Fuller, "Canada and the 'Buffalo,' *Bison bison*: A Tale of Two Herds," *Canadian Field-Naturalist* 116 (Jan.–Mar. 2002), 152.

89. Maxwell Graham, "Finding Range for Canada's Buffalo," *Canadian Field-Naturalist* 38 (Dec. 1924), 189.

90. UAA, Memorandum from Maxwell Graham, 19 Mar. 1919, Buffalo National Park Files, 2002-18-4.

91. John Sandlos, "Where the Scientists Roam: Ecology, Management and Bison in Northern Canada," *Journal of Canadian Studies* 37 (Summer 2002): 99.

92. Quoted in Sandlos, "Where the Scientists Roam," 100.

93. Sandlos, "Where the Scientists Roam," 100.

94. Maxwell Graham, *Canada's Wild Buffalo: Observations in the Wood Buffalo Park, 1922* (Ottawa 1923), 12.

95. Maxwell Graham, *Canada's Wild Buffalo*, 8. It was believed that once introduced into the environment of the wood bison, the plains bison would begin to take on some of the characteristics of the wood bison. Such was substantiated by J. D. Soper, a naturalist/explorer who was appointed in 1934 as Dominion Wildlife Officer for the Prairies. J. Alexander Burnett, "A Passion for Wildlife: A History of the Canadian Wildlife Service, 1947–1997," *Canadian Field-Naturalist*, 113 (Jan.– Mar. 1999), 13. Soper reported that environmental conditions were affecting the plains bison that had been transferred to Wood Buffalo National Park. He reported, "The 'Wainwrights' are becoming increasingly sturdier, heavier, and [get] darker pelts as the years go by." UAA, Summary of correspondence dealing with the transfer of the buffalo from Wainwright to Wood Buffalo Park, 6 May 1933, Buffalo National Park Files, 2002-18-1.

96. Maxwell Graham, *Canada's Wild Buffalo*, 12.

97. Maxwell Graham, "Finding Range for Canada's Buffalo," *Canadian Field-Naturalist*, 38 (Dec. 1924), 189. It is quite possible that Graham relied on information from a report by F. B. Siebert. During the 1922 boundary survey "on his reconnaissance of the home of the Wood Buffalo," Siebert stated that while it was possible for bison from northern and southern herds to mingle, the two herds did not seem to unite. UAA, Summary of the correspondence on file giving reasons for introducing the Wainwright bison to the Wood Buffalo Park and the representations made by those who were opposed to such action, 1926, Buffalo National Park Files, 2002-18-1.

98. In 1910, Harry V. Radford collected information on the wood bison and its habitat. He also procured a specimen and compared this animal with its plains counterpart. When compared to the plains bison that had been killed by William Hornaday, which held the world record for bison in size and weight, the wood bison was remarkably bigger in proportion; Radford declared it the largest wild animal to be killed in North or South America. LAC, H. V. Radford to Colonel Fred White, 12 Feb. 1910, Parks Canada Files, BNP, RG 84, Vol. 58, BU299-2, pt. 1.

	Hornaday's plains bison killed 6 Dec. 1896	Radford's wood bison killed 1 Dec. 1909
Total weight	2,100 LBS (EST.)	2,402 LBS
Height at shoulder	5 FT. 8 IN.	5 FT. 10 IN.
Length of head and body to root of tail	10 FT. 2 IN.	9 FT. 7 IN.
Length of tail vertebrae	1 FT. 3 IN.	1 FT. 7½ IN.
Girth behind forelegs	8 FT. 4 IN.	9 FT. 9 IN.
Circumference of muzzle behind nostrils	2 FT. 2 IN.	2 FT. 3 5/8 IN.

99. Francis Harper, "Correspondence," *Canadian Field-Naturalist* 39 (Feb. 1925), 45.

100. Harper, "Correspondence," 45.

101. W. E. Saunders and A. Brozier Howell, "Correspondence," *Canadian Field-Naturalist* 39 (May 1925), 118.

102. LAC, W. T. Hornaday to Francis Harper, 17 Mar. 1925, Parks Canada Files, BNP, RG 84, Vol. 58, BU299-2, pt. 1.

103. LAC, W. T. Hornaday to Francis Harper, 17 Mar. 1925, Parks Canada Files, BNP, RG 84, Vol. 58, BU299-2, pt. 1.

104. Burnett, "A Passion for Wildlife," 12.

105. Lothian, *A History of Canada's National Parks*, 34.

106. UAA, Summary of correspondence dealing with the transfer of the buffalo from Wainwright to Wood Buffalo Park, 6 May 1933, Buffalo National Park Files, 2002-18-1, UAA.

107. LAC, A. G. Smith to Commissioner, 17 Dec. 1923, Parks Canada Files, BNP, RG 84, Vol. 58, BU299-2, pt. 1.

108. LAC, Richard Waddy to Veterinary Director General, 7 Jan. 1924, Parks Canada Files, BNP, RG 84, Vol. 58, BU299-2, pt. 1.

109. UAA, Summary of correspondence dealing with the transfer of the buffalo from Wainwright to Wood Buffalo Park, 6 May 1933, Buffalo National Park Files, 2002-18-1.

110. LAC, Quoted in A. G. Smith to O. S. Finnie, 7 Jul. 1925, Parks Canada Files, BNP, RG 84, Vol. 52, BU232-1 pt. 2.

111. LAC, O. S. Finnie to F. H. H. Williamson, 3 Mar. 1926 and A. G. Smith to the Commissioner, 12 May 1926, Parks Canada Files, BNP, RG 84, Vol. 52, BU232-1 pt. 2.

112. Ray Sharp, interview.

113. Harold Shepstone devotes one chapter of his book *Wild Beasts Today* to the demise and salvage efforts of the Dominion government. He concludes his chapter with details of the transfer of the plains bison from Wainwright. He portrays the scheme in a positive light, stating that the herd at Wood Buffalo National Park would soon be used to supply meat and leather products to Canadians. Harold J. Shepstone, *Wild Beasts Today* (London 1931), 126–34.

114. UAA, Summary of correspondence dealing with the transfer of the buffalo from Wainwright to Wood Buffalo Park, 6 May 1933, Buffalo National Park Files, 2002-18-1.

115. UAA, Summary of correspondence, 6 May 1933, Buffalo National Park Files, 2002-18-1.

116. Fuller, "Canada and the 'Buffalo,'" 155–56; Burnett, "A Passion for Wildlife," 15.

The Forgotten Park

ON THE EVE OF THE PARK'S CLOSURE IN 1939, the *Ottawa Evening Journal* reported:

> The range at Wainwright Park, it is explained by those who should know, has deteriorated greatly in recent years. The soil is light, and through over-grazing the natural pasturage has been replaced to a considerable extent by non-edible plants, and the natural feed of the herds has had to be supplemented. Thus the enterprise ceased to be a conservation project under natural conditions but an exhibition herd partly maintained out of public funds."[1]

Although the journalist implied that the effort at one time occurred under natural conditions, evidence shows that from the onset there was nothing natural about the Buffalo National Park effort to save the bison. The growth of the herd had disastrous consequences. The deterioration of the range exhausted the natural forage that the bison required. However, the increasing prevalence of tuberculosis among the bison and other animals left the Parks Branch little choice but to take drastic measures and close the park.

The Park's closure caught those working at the park by surprise. Superintendent A. G. Smith did not receive word until October of that year that all the animals were to be slaughtered, and he notified the wardens and other park employees shortly after.[2] The last roundup of the bison, an event that has become legendary in local history, took place in 1939 and the moose, elk, and deer were disposed of in early 1940.[3] While there was some talk of reinstating the area as a national park following the war[4] financial considerations decided the issue. The Dominion government was no longer interested in maintaining the park and said the expense could not be justified when the preservation of the bison had been "amply accomplished" with healthy bison in Elk Island National Park as well as bison in Riding Mountain and Wood Buffalo National Parks.[5] An arrangement was made between the federal and provincial governments to relinquish Buffalo National Park to the Department of National Defence in exchange for 24 sections of land in the Cooking Lake Forest Reserve to be added to Elk Island National Park to expand the bison effort there.[6] Buffalo National Park was officially abolished by an act of Parliament in 1947.[7] The cattalo experiment, which had been allowed to remain in the area, was moved in 1950 to the Dominion Range Experiment Station in Manyberries, Alberta.[8]

The official position, written in an article entitled "Canada's Buffalo Herds" by the publicity division of the Parks Branch, stated that overgrazing, due to the increase of the herd, had resulted in unanticipated problems. "Naturally, the Government does not wish to engage in large-scale farming operations to supplement food supplies of animals which should be self-supporting. To do so would be to change the whole character of the enterprise."[9] Those who inquired about the closure were informed that the decision was made with a sense of duty to the interest of taxpayers. "No admission fee is charged at Buffalo Park, Wainwright, and yet the record of attendance does not show widespread interest, consequently it would be difficult to maintain that the park is a valuable factor from a tourist standpoint."[10]

However, this official position masked two greater reasons for the park's closure. With the Second World War looming, a better use had been found for the area than a wildlife reserve. The Department of National Defence, looking for an expanse of land for manoeuvring and training troops and artillery use,[11] had expressed an interest in obtaining the area. Indeed, the government saw the Department of National Defence's interest in the area as fortuitous. It allowed them to maintain credibility, as they did not want the diseased state of the herd to be publicized. As the director of the Department of Mines and Resources remarked, "The outstanding feature of the whole matter from our standpoint is that the present is the first opportunity we have had to wind up affairs at Wainwright without admitting publicly that the herd was in bad condition."[12]

Some, like J. R. Dymond, the chair of the Ecological Society of America, however, criticized the Parks Branch for not disclosing the true reasons for the park's closure. His criticism is perhaps indicative of how much the understanding of the idea conservation had evolved since Buffalo National Park had opened and how damning the news of the failed effort to save the bison would be if the truth were revealed to the public. He stated:

I consider the most unfortunate feature of this affair is not the destruction of the buffalo herd which can be built up again but the demonstration to the public that a national park can be wiped out without giving the public any convincing evidence for the necessity for the action…the destruction of Buffalo Park is, so far as the public's information is concerned in direct contradiction of most of the principles which they have been told underlie the establishment of parks. Perhaps the public has been oversold on National Parks but the fact remains that most conservationists have been stunned by the announcement about Buffalo Park and I am afraid it will do a great deal of harm to the national park idea in Canada.[13]

The story of Buffalo National Park is not about the saving of a near extinct species, but that the effort had gone so terribly wrong it was forced to close after only three decades. A century after Buffalo National Park was established, the bison at Wainwright are all but forgotten. However, it appears that shortly after the bison were purchased, this park was also forgotten by the very group who had established it. The Dominion government, which at the turn of the century was eager to acquire the bison herd and approved an additional $100,000 to purchase them, seemed to believe that the herd would need little management. As was proved early on, the park could not be self-sufficient and there was no plan in place or money designated to ensure the bison salvage effort could operate effectively. The annual maintenance of the park was $45,000 to $50,000.[14] By the time of the park's closure, the total revenue obtained by the park was approximately one third of the expenditures that the effort had incurred.[15]

Buffalo National Park was both a product and a victim of the cultural forces of the early 20th century. Ideas and trends of this era and the political and economic climate of the nation influenced and shaped the bison-saving effort at Wainwright but also contributed to its downfall. Romantic sentiment for the near-extinct plains bison and a spirit of competition drove the Dominion government to purchase the Pablo bison herd. These motives, however, overshadowed the effort to preserve the species. The development of Buffalo National Park was modelled after the mountain parks, but this touristic template was not transferable to a prairie park. While Buffalo National Park was successful at breeding bison and game, the necessity of confining the animals to the park quickly proved too much for the land base to support.

Little was known of wildlife management when Buffalo National Park was established, so administrators were treading in unfamiliar territory. Lack of federal funding to operate the park after it was established, however, contributed greatly to the downfall of the park. Administrators in the Parks Branch, a minor branch of the federal government, were not given the resources or authority to manage the bison-saving effort effectively. While the calamities that troubled the park can, in part, be blamed on this ignorance of wildlife management, the disinterest of the Dominion government served to make the problems much worse. If the government had intervened when it first learned of the seriousness of the situation at Wainwright, perhaps the crises could have been avoided. With little support and no revenue, the Parks Branch had to find ways to solve the park's problems and make the effort pay for itself. Very quickly, the commercial value of the herd superseded the concern of ensuring the future of the species.

Despite the economic strain they were under, the administration in the Parks Branch also showed poor judgement in their management decisions. The most poignant example is the decision to ship a diseased bison herd north to Wood Buffalo National Park, which was done against the protest of leading experts and even some individuals within the Parks Branch. Management decisions to curtail the exploding population of the bison herd were not driven by a preservation ethic, or even any consistent principle, but instead were stop-gap measures to deal with the mounting problems at the park. The decision to close Buffalo National Park in 1939 seems in hindsight to be one of the wisest decisions made in the name of conservation.

Does the story of Buffalo National Park have any relevance today? Parks Canada officials have had no success purging the Wood Buffalo National Park hybrid wood/plains bison herd of tuberculosis—a problem that is the direct result of the decision to ship the Wainwright plains bison north. Biologist William A. Fuller has suggested that the compromised herd be slaughtered and a new herd built up using the disease-free wood bison from the Mackenzie Bison Sanctuary.[16] He notes that in 1990, the Report of the Environmental Panel on Northern Diseased Bison called for a complete slaughter of all the bison in Wood Buffalo National Park.[17] In 2006, the Canadian government was still considering a plan to cull the bison herd and repopulate the area with wood buffalo from Elk Island National Park.[18] To date there has been no movement on this proposal. In Wood Buffalo National Park, the history of Buffalo National Park lives on.

As recently as March 2008, the problems of disease and lack of range has posed problems for the management of the bison herd in Yellowstone National Park in the US states of Wyoming, Montana, and Idaho. Public protests over the lack of federal funding to increase the territory for the bison and culling of the herd, as well as concerns that the bison could spread brucellosis to the cattle populations outside the park, sound strangely like déjà vu.[19] Lessons need to be learned from the problems and failures experienced by Buffalo National Park to prevent similar consequences in our wildlife preservation efforts today.

Notes

1. *Ottawa Evening Journal*, 5 Dec. 1939 "The Wainwright Buffalo," LAC, Parks Canada Files, Buffalo National Park [BNP], RG 84, Vol. 50, File BU2, pt. 1.

2. LAC, F. H. H. Williamson to Superintendent, 18 Oct. 1939, Parks Canada Files, BNP, RG 84, Vol. 58, File BU299, pt. 15; Ray Sharp, interview.

3. Lothian, *A History of Canada's National Parks*, 37.

4. LAC, R. A. Gibson to Colonel H. DesRosiers, 20 Oct. 1941, Parks Canada Files, BNP, RG 84, Vol. 982, File BU2[548608], pt. 4.

5. LAC, Notes for File Bu. 2, Reference to Buffalo Park in Hansard and summary of discussions at Session 1940, 29 Aug. 1940, Parks Canada Files, BNP, RG 84, Vol. 982, File BU2[548608], pt. 4.

6. LAC, "Re: Buffalo National Park," n.d, W. J. F. Pratt to J. P. Tripp, 6 Apr. 1947, and Buffalo National Park, 15 Apr. 1947, Parks Canada Files, BNP, RG 84, Vol. 982, File BU2[548608], pt. 4.

7. *National Parks Amendment Act*, S.C. 1947, c. 66, s. 6.

8. LAC, F. K. Kristjansson, "An Evaluation of the Potentialities of the 'Cattalo' Project with Special Reference to Reproduction Problems," 19 Feb. 1952, Department of Agriculture Files, Cattalo, RG 17, Vol. 3456, File 30-9-1(1).

9. LAC, R. A. Gibson to the Deputy Minister and Mr. Williamson, 22 Dec. 1939 and *Canada's Buffalo Herds*, Parks Canada Files, BNP, RG 84, Vol. 982, File BU2[548608], pt. 3.

10. LAC, F. H. H. Williamson to R. W. Tufts, 28 Dec. 1939 and "Sample" form letter. Parks Canada Files, BNP, RG 84, Vol. 982, File BU2[548608], pt. 3.

11. LAC, "Re: Buffalo National Park," n.d., and Notes for File BU. 2, References to Buffalo Park in Hansard and summary of discussions at Session 1940, Parks Canada Files, BNP, RG 84, Vol. 982, File BU2[548608], pt. 4.

12. LAC, Director of the Department of Mines and Resources to the Deputy Minister, 28 Sept. 1939, Parks Canada Files, BNP, RG 84, Vol. 982, File BU2 [548608], pt. 2.

13. LAC, J. R. Dymond to F. H. H. Williamson, 23 Nov. 1939, Parks Canada Files, BNP, RG 84, Vol. 982, File BU2[548608], pt. 3.

14. Notes for File BU. 2, References to Buffalo Park in Hansard and summary of discussions at Session 1940.

15. LAC, Controller to Mr. Gibson, 7 Dec. 1943, Parks Canada Files, BNP, RG 84, Vol. 982, File BU2[548608], pt. 4.

16. While it was believed that the transfer of the plains bison herd had wiped out the wood bison species, a miraculous discovery was made in 1958. Dr. N. S. Novakowski stumbled across what he believed to be a pure wood bison herd in a secluded corner along the northern border of Wood Buffalo National Park. After eliminating those that reacted to tuberculosis and brucellosis tests, the herd was split. Eighteen were moved to Ft. Providence north of the Mackenzie River, and the remaining animals were sent to Elk Island National Park. Fuller states that while the validity of the claims that the animals were pure wood bison has been debated since, he believes that these bison are "the closest we will ever see to the original Wood Bison." Fuller, "Canada and the 'Buffalo,'" 157.

17. Fuller, "Canada and the 'Buffalo,'" 158.

18. *Calgary Herald*, 20 Mar. 2006, Ed Struzik, "Diseased Bison Face Massive Cull."

19. *New York Times*, 23 Mar. 2008, Jim Robbins, "Anger Over Culling of Yellowstone's Bison."

Bibliography

ARCHIVAL PRIMARY SOURCES

Battle River Historical Society Photograph Collection.
Home of the Buffalo. VHS. With commentary by Ray Sharp. n.d.

Brower Photograph Collection
Private Collection.

Buffalo National Park Foundation
Archives
Davison fonds
Rutherford fonds
Sharp, Ray. Interview, circa 2001

Glenbow Archives
Photograph Collection
Ribstone Creek Sheet. Map. G3471, G4, s380, 266.

Library and Archives of Canada
Parks Canada Files. Buffalo National Park. RG 84, Vols. 50–57, 155, 981–982. Department of Agriculture Files. Cattalo. RG 17, Vols. 1249 and 3456.

Provincial Archives of Alberta
Dominion Land Surveyor Records. File 83.376.

Snyder Photograph Collection
Private Collection.

Treffry Photograph Collection
Private Collection

University of Alberta Archives
Buffalo National Park Files. 2002-18.

William C. Wonders Map Collection, University of Alberta
Buffalo Park. Map. Canada. G-9 Buffalo Park (1926).

PUBLISHED PRIMARY SOURCES

Benham, D. J. "The Round Up of the Second Herd of Pablo's Buffalo." *Edmonton Bulletin*, 8 Nov. 1907, 9–11.

Boyd, Mossom M. "Crossing Bison and Cattle." *Journal of Heredity* 5 (1914), 189–97.

Buffalo Trails and Tales. n.p., Giltedge Ladies Booster Club, 1973.

Butler, William Francis. *The Great Lone Land: A Narrative of Travel and Adventure in the North-West of America.* Edmonton: M. G. Hurtig, 1968.

Cameron, A. E. "Some Further Notes on Buffalo." *Veterinary Journal* 80 (1924), 413–17.

Canada: Its History, Productions and Natural Resources. Ottawa: Department of Agriculture, 1886. Rev. eds. 1904, 1906.

Cotton, E. J. (Bud). *Buffalo Bud: Adventures of a Cowboy.* Vancouver: Hancock House Publishers, 1981.

———. "Range Riding with Canada's Buffalo Herds." Unpublished manuscript, Personal collection of Adeline Schleppe, n.d.

Deakin, A., G. W. Muir, and A. G. Smith. *Hybridization of Domestic Cattle, Bison and Yak.* Ottawa: Department of Agriculture, 1935.

Dixon, Herb. Personal Interview. 12 Feb. 2004.

Elrod, Morton J. "The Flathead Buffalo Range." *Annual Report of the American Bison Society, 1905–1907.* 15–49. n.p.: American Bison Society, 1908.

Goodnight, Charles. "My Experience with Bison Hybrids." *Journal of Heredity* 5 (1914): 197–99.

Goodnight's American Buffalo Ranch, Goodnight Texas. Dallas: H. A. Fleming, 1910.

Graham, Maxwell. *Canada's Wild Buffalo: Observations in the Wood Buffalo Park, 1922.* Ottawa: King's Printer, 1923.

———. "Finding Range for Canada's Buffalo." *Canadian Field-Naturalist,* 38 (Dec. 1924), 189.

Grant, Johnny. *Very Close to Trouble: The Johnny Grant Memoir* / edited with historical annotations by Lyndel Meikle, Pullman: Washington State University Press, 1996.

Grinnell, George Bird. "The Last of the Buffalo." *Scribner's Magazine* 12 (Sept. 1892), 267–86.

Grinnell, George Bird and Charles Sheldon, eds. *Hunting and Conservation: The Book of the Boone and Crockett Club.* New Haven: Yale University Press, 1925.

Harper, Francis. "Correspondence." *Canadian Field-Naturalist* 39 (Feb. 1925), 45.

Hendry, Anthony. *The Journal of Anthony Hendry, 1754–55: York Factory to the Blackfeet Country.* Lawrence J. Burpee, ed. Toronto: Canadiana House, 1973.

Hewitt, C. Gordon. "The Coming Back of the Bison." *Natural History* 19 (Dec. 1919), 553–565.

———. "Conservation, or the Protection of Nature." *The Ottawa Naturalist,* 24 (March, 1911), 209–221.

———. *The Conservation of the Wild Life of Canada.* New York: Charles Scribner's Sons, 1921.

Hind, Henry Youle. *British North America Reports of Progress Together with a Preliminary and General Report on the Assiniboine and Saskatchewan Exploring Expedition.* London: George Edward Eyre and William Spottiswoode, 1860.

———. *Narrative of the Canadian Red River Exploring Expedition of 1857 and the Assiniboine and Saskatchewan Exploring Expeditions of 1858.* 2 vols. London: Longman, Green, Longman, and Roberts, 1860.

Hornaday, William Temple. *The Extermination of the American Bison.* Washington: Smithsonian Institution Press, 2002.

Howell, A. Brozier. "Correspondence." *Canadian Field-Naturalist* 39 (May 1925), 118.

Jones, C. J. "Breeding Cattalo." *American Breeder's Association Annual Report* 3 (1907), 161–65.

———. "My Buffalo Experiments." *Independent* 60 (1906), 1351–55.

Journals, Detailed Reports, and Observations Relative to the Exploration by Captain Palliser, of that Portion of British North America, which, in Latitude Lies Between the British Boundary Line and the Height of Land of Watershed of the Northern or Frozen Ocean Respectively, and in Longitude, Between the Western Shore of Lake Superior and the Pacific Ocean During the Years 1857, 1858, 1859, and 1860. London: George Edward Eyre and William Spottiswoode, 1863.

Kelsey, Henry. *The Kelsey Papers*. Regina: Canadian Plains Research Center, 1994.

Longstaff, Alan N. "Evolving the Arctic Cow." *Maclean's Magazine*, 15 Jan. 1927.

Macoun, John. *Manitoba and the Great North-West: The Field for Investment; The Home of the Emigrant*. London: T. C. Jack, 1883.

National Parks Act, Statutes of Canada 1930, c. 33, s. 4.

National Parks Amendment Act, Statutes of Canada 1947, c. 66, s. 6.

Nelson, Jorgen. "How Practical Are Cattalo? Buffalo and Domestic Cattle Have Long Been Crossbred." *American Feed and Grain Dealer* 30 (Sept. 1946), 8–9, 27, 42.

"New Warden Appointed Wainwright Buffalo Pk." *Wainwright Star*, 23 Aug. 1939.

North West of Canada: A General Sketch of the Extent, Woods and Forests, Mineral Resources and Climatology of the Four Provisional Districts of Assiniboia, Saskatchewan, Alberta and Athabasca. Ottawa: Department of Agriculture, 1887.

Palliser, John. *The Papers of the Palliser Expedition, 1857–1860*. Irene M. Spry, ed. Toronto: Champlain Society, 1968.

Palliser, John, James Hector, and J. W. Sullivan. "Progress of the British North American Exploring Expedition." *Journal of the Royal Geographical Society of London* 30 (1860), 267–314.

Peters, H. F. *Range Experimental Farm, Manyberries, Alberta, Progress Report, 1948–1953*. Ottawa: Experimental Farms Service, Department of Agriculture, 1955.

Reindeer and Musk-Ox: Report of the Royal Commission upon the Possibilities of the Reindeer and Musk-Ox Industries in the Arctic and Sub-Arctic Regions. Ottawa: Department of the Interior, 1922.

"Report Shows Buffalo Increase." *Wainwright Star*, 15 May 1918.

Rocky Mountains Park Act, Statutes of Canada 1887, c. 32, s. 4.

Rothwell, G. B. *Report of the Dominion Animal Husbandman for the Year Ending March 31, 1924*. Ottawa: Department of Agriculture, 1925.

Saunders W. E. "Correspondence." *Canadian Field-Naturalist* 39 (May 1925), 118.

Schleppe, Adeline. Personal Interview. 11 Nov. 2002.

Shepstone, Harold J. *Wild Beasts Today*. London: Sampson Low, Marston, 1931.

Sifton, Clifford. *Review of Work of the Commission of Conservation*. Montreal: Federated Press, 1917.

Thompson, David. *David Thompson's Narrative of His Explorations in Western America, 1784–1812*. J. B. Tyrrell, ed. Toronto: Champlain Society, 1916.

Thompson, Ernest E. "A List of the Mammals of Manitoba." *Transactions of the Manitoba Scientific and Historical Society* 23 (May 1886).

Transactions of the Ethnological Society of London. Vol. 1. London: John Murray, 1861.

Treffry, Ellis. Personal Interview. 11 Nov. 2002.

Wainwright Star, 15 May 1918.

Williams, M. B. *Guardians of the Wild*. London: Thomas Nelson and Sons, 1936.

SECONDARY SOURCES

Altmeyer, George. "Three Ideas of Nature in Canada, 1893–1914." In Chad Gaffield and Pam Gaffield, eds., *Consuming Canada: Readings in Environmental History*. Toronto: Copp Clark, 1995, 96–118.

Arthur, George W. *An Introduction to the Ecology of the Early Historic Communal Bison Hunting Among the Northern Plains Indians*. Ottawa: National Museums of Canada, 1975.

Bamforth, Douglas B. *Ecology and Human Organization on the Great Plains*. New York: Plenum Press, 1988.

Bella, Leslie. *Parks for Profit*. Montreal: Harvest House, 1987.

Binnema, Theodore. *Common and Contested Ground: A Human and Environmental History of the Northwestern Plains*. Norman: University of Oklahoma Press, 2001.

Brink, Jack. *Dog Days in Southern Alberta*. Edmonton: Alberta Culture Historical Resources Division, 1986.

Brown, Robert Craig. "The Doctrine of Usefulness: Natural Resource and National Park Policy in Canada, 1887–1914." In J. G. Nelson, ed., *Canadian Parks in Perspective*. Montreal: Harvest House, 1968, 46–62.

Budd, Archibald C. and Keith F. Best, *Wild Plants of the Canadian Prairies*. Ottawa: Research Branch, Canada Department of Agriculture, 1969.

Burnett, J. Alexander, ed. "A Passion for Wildlife: A History of the Canadian Wildlife Service, 1947–1997." Special issue, *Canadian Field-Naturalist* 113 (Jan.–Mar. 1999).

Burns, Robert J. *Guardians of the Wild: A History of the Warden Service of Canada's National Parks*. Calgary: University of Calgary Press, 2000.

Coder, George David. "The National Movement to Preserve the American Buffalo in the United States and Canada Between 1880 and 1920." Ph.D. diss., Ohio State University, 1975.

Colpitts, George. *Game in the Garden: A Human History of Wildlife in Western Canada to 1940*. Vancouver: University of British Columbia Press, 2002.

Cronon, William. *Changes in the Land: Indians, Colonists, and the Ecology of New England*. New York: Hill and Wang, 1983.

Dunlap, Thomas R. "Ecology, Nature, and Canadian National Park Policy: Wolves, Elk, and Bison as a Case Study." In Rowland Lorimer et al., eds., *To See Ourselves/To Save Ourselves: Ecology and Culture in Canada*. Montreal: Association for Canadian Studies, 1991, 139–47

———. *Saving America's Wildlife*. Princeton: Princeton University Press, 1988.

"Flathead Reservation Timeline." *Flathead Reservation Historical Society*, Montana Heritage Project, 2004. <http://www.flatheadreservation.org/timeline/timeline.html> (14 Jun. 2004).

Foster, Janet. *Working for Wildlife: The Beginning of Preservation in Canada*. 2nd ed. Toronto: University of Toronto Press, 1998.

Foster, John E. "Introduction." In John Foster, Dick Harrison, and I. S. MacLaren, eds., *Buffalo*. Edmonton: University of Alberta Press, 1992, vii–xi.

Francis, R. Douglas. "Changing Images of the West." In R. Douglas Francis and Howard Palmer, eds., *The Prairie West: Historical Readings*. Edmonton: Pica Pica Press, 1985, 629–49.

Fuller, W. A. "Canada and the 'Buffalo,' *Bison bison*: A Tale of Two Herds." *Canadian Field-Naturalist* 116 (Jan.– Mar. 2002), 141–59.

Gillis, R. Peter, and Thomas R. Roach. "The American Influence on Conservation in Canada: 1899–1911." *Journal of Forest History* 30 (Oct. 1986), 160–174.

——. "The Beginnings of a Movement: The Montreal Congress and its Aftermath, 1880–1896." In Chad Gaffield and Pam Gaffield, eds., *Consuming Canada: Readings in Environmental History*. Toronto: Copp Clark, 1995, 131–51.

Hays, Samuel P. *Conservation and the Gospel of Efficiency: The Progressive Conservation Movement, 1890–1920*. Cambridge: Harvard University Press, 1959.

Isenberg, Andrew. "The Returns of the Bison: Nostalgia, Profit, and Preservation." *Environmental History* 2 (Apr. 1997), 179–96.

Isenberg, Andrew C. *The Destruction of the Bison*. Cambridge: Cambridge University Press, 2000.

Kaye, B., and D. W. Moodie. "Geographical Perspectives on the Canadian Plains." In Richard Allen, ed., *A Region of the Mind*. Regina: Canadian Plains Research Center, 1973, 7–46.

Locke, Harvey, and Dave Poulton. "Campaigns." *CPAWS Calgary*. <www.cpawscalgary.org/national-parks/protect-parks.html> (20 Jan. 2003).

Loo, Tina. "Making a Modern Wilderness: Conserving Wildlife in Twentieth-Century Canada." *Canadian Historical Review* 82 (March 2001), 92–121.

——. *States of Nature: Conserving Canada's Wildlife in the Twentieth Century*. Vancouver: UBC Press, 2006.

Lothian, W. F. *A History of Canada's National Parks*. Vol. 4. Ottawa: Indian and Northern Affairs, Parks Canada, 1981.

Lott, Dale F. *American Bison: A Natural History*. Berkeley: University of California Press, 2002.

MacDonald, Graham. *Science and History at Elk Island: Conservation Work in a Canadian National Park: 1914–1994*. Calgary: Historical Services Parks Canada, 1994.

MacEachern, Alan. "The Conservation Movement." In *Canada, Confederation to Present* [CD-ROM]. Bob Hesketh and Chris Hackett, eds., Edmonton: Chinook Multimedia, 2001.

——. *Natural Selections: National Parks in Atlantic Canada, 1935–1970*. Montreal: McGill-Queens University Press, 2001.

MacLaren, I. S. "Buffalo in Word and Image: From European Origins to the Art of Clarence Tillenius." In John Foster, Dick Harrison, and I. S. MacLaren, eds., *Buffalo*. Edmonton, University of Alberta Press, 1992, 79–129.

McNamee, Kevin. "From Wild Places to Endangered Spaces: A History of Canada's National Parks." In Philip Dearden and Rick Rollins, eds., *Parks and Protected Areas in Canada: Planning and Management*. Toronto: Oxford University Press, 1993, 17–44.

Martin, Paul S., and Christine R. Szuter. "War Zones and Game Sinks in Lewis and Clark's West." *Conservation Biology* 13 (February 1999), 36–45.

Marty, Sid. *A Grand and Fabulous Notion: The First Century of Canada's Parks*. Toronto: NC Press, 1984.

Morton, W. L. *Henry Youle Hind, 1823–1908*. Toronto: University of Toronto Press, 1980.

Nash, Roderick, ed. *The American Environment: Readings in the History of Conservation*. Massachusetts: Addison-Wesley Publishing, 1968.

Nash, Roderick Frazier. *Wilderness and the American Mind*. 4th ed. New Haven: Yale University Press, 2001.

"Natural Wonders & Cultural Treasures." *Elk Island National Park of Canada*. <http://www2.parkscanada. gc.ca/pn-np/ab/elkisland/natcul/ natcul1biii_E.asp> (30 March 2008).

Ogilvie, Sheilagh C. *The Park Buffalo*. Calgary: National and Provincial Parks Association of Canada, 1979.

Owram, Doug. *Promise of Eden: The Canadian Expansionist Movement and the Idea of the West, 1856–1900*. Toronto: University of Toronto Press, 1980.

Potyondi, Barry. *Wood Buffalo National Park: An Historical Overview and Source Study*. Parks Canada: 1979.

Potyondi, Barry, and D. M. Loveridge. *From Wood Mountain to the Whitemud: A Historical Survey of the Grasslands National Park Area*. Ottawa: Parks Canada and Environment Canada, 1983.

Reiger, John F. *American Sportsmen and the Origins of Conservation*. New York: Winchester Press, 1975.

Roe, F. G. *The North American Buffalo: A Critical Study of the Species in its Wild State*. 2nd ed. Toronto: University of Toronto Press, 1970.

Robbins, Jim. "Anger Over Culling of Yellowstone's Bison." *New York Times*, 23 Mar. 2008.

Runte, Alfred. *National Parks: The American Experience*. Lincoln: University of Nebraska Press, 1979.

Russo, John P. *The Kaibab North Deer Herd: Its History, Problems and Management*. Phoenix: State of Arizona Game and Fish Department, 1964.

Sandlos, John. "Where the Scientists Roam: Ecology, Management and Bison in Northern Canada." *Journal of Canadian Studies* 37 (Summer 2002), 93–130.

Schama, Simon. *Landscape and Memory*. New York: Alfred A. Knopf, 1995.

Scribner, Marsha. *Transitions: Commemorating Camp Wainwright's 50th Anniversary*. n.p.: Jostens, 1990.

Sellers, Richard. *Preserving Nature in the National Parks: A History*. New Haven: Yale University Press, 1997.

Spry, Irene. "The Great Transformation: The Disappearance of the Commons in Western Canada." In Richard Allen, ed., *Man and Nature on the Prairies*. Regina: Canadian Plains Research Center, 1976, 21–45.

Struzik, Ed. "Diseased Bison Face Massive Cull." *Calgary Herald*, 20 Mar. 2006.

Taylor, C. J. "Legislating Nature: The National Parks Act of 1930." In Rowland Lorimer et al., eds., *To See Ourselves/To Save Ourselves: Ecology and Culture in Canada*. Montreal: Association for Canadian Studies, 1991, 125–37.

Trefethen, James B. *An American Crusade for Wildlife*. New York: Winchester Press and the Boone and Crockett Club, 1975.

Vickers, J. Roderick. *Alberta Plains Prehistory: A Review*. Edmonton: Alberta Culture Historical Resources Division, 1986.

Warkentin, John, ed. *The Western Interior of Canada: A Record of Geographical Discovery 1612 to 1917*. Toronto: McClelland and Stewart, 1964.

Warkentin, John. "Steppe, Desert and Empire." In A. W. Rasporich and H. C. Klassen, eds., *Prairie Perspectives 2*. Toronto: Holt, Rinehart, and Winston, 1973, 102–36.

Whealdon, Bon I. et al. *I Will Be Meat for My Salish: The Montana Writers Project and the Buffalo of the Flathead Indian Reservation*. Pablo: Salish Kootenai College, 2001.

Wilson, Michael Clayton. "Bison in Alberta: Paleontology, Evolution, and Relationships with Humans." In John Foster, Dick Harrison, and I. S. MacLaren, eds., *Buffalo*. Edmonton: University of Alberta Press, 1992, 1–17.

Wonders, Karen. "A Sportsman's Eden: A Wilderness Beckons." Pt. 1. *Beaver* 79 (Oct./Nov. 1999), 26–32.

———. "A Sportsman's Eden: A Wilderness Besieged." Pt. 2. *Beaver* 79 (Dec. 1999–Jan. 2000), 30–37.

Worster, Donald. "Doing Environmental History." In Chad Gaffield and Pam Gaffield, eds., *Consuming Canada: Readings in Environmental History*. Toronto: Copp Clark, 1995, 16–32.

Wyatt, F. A., and J. D. Newton et al. *Soil Survey of Wainwright and Vermilion Sheets*. Edmonton: University of Alberta, 1944.

Zeller, Suzanne. *Inventing Canada: Early Victorian Science and the Idea of a Transcontinental Nation*. Toronto: University of Toronto Press, 1987.

Index